trambles

I0487010

tr.

**There is
an increasing
variety of
art galleries
and public art
across London.
Make the most
of opportunities
to view exhibitions
on art rambles
or 'trambles'
See more art
Stopping
for tea
cake and
perhaps
an occasional beer
along the way.**

**Become a trambler,
and discover
London's art on foot.**

Take plenty of fresh fruit,
oat biscuits, ginger cake,
water, camera, lens cloth,
pen, pencils, sharpener,
eraser, notebook
sketchbook, umbrella,
hat, gloves, search engine
or map

Often when visiting cities the temptation is to keep pace with the city itself. Once the major sights have all been ticked, it's on to the next one.
This guide aims to take you to the next level. On trambles or 'art rambles' discover public art and art galleries around each corner These tried and tested routes take you behind the major sights.
Like being behind the scenes on a grand film set. With discoveries and photo opportunities along the way. trambles are the best way to discover London and see more art, on foot. This guide is also packed with recommendations from bookshops to cinemas, places to eat and a few of the more unusual places that are unique to London.

5

Not to be confused with:

Mooch
Another enjoyable city pastime, but tends to take place inside London's remaining record shops and bookstores. Moochers stay happily indoors for hours on end, often unaware of a change in the weather. Tend to wear those large headphones that are difficult to see past.

Meander
A winding walk with no intention, a pleasant stroll but not informative. The intention of Trambles is learning more about art and the city.

Pub Crawls
A pint at the end of a tramble or a half along the way is a real treat. However several pints may spoil the pleasure of trambling. Extended pub-crawls may end up with participant's in silly head gear

Ramble
On green hills in the country. Often involves drinking tepid tea from flasks, Aran jumpers, woolly hats, shorts and brightly coloured socks rolled down over walking boots. Quite different to trambles!

Surfing
A surfer's loose fitting baggy clothes, and lazy sway back does not suit trambles. Street Surfers and Skaters weaving on wheels can distract a trambler from seeing around them.
The net is great for research, but when it comes to viewing art, nothing beats getting up close to the real thing.

Breughel on Google? Rothko on a Nokia? I don't think so!
n.b. the net is not to be confused with the back of a goal, where the ball has to be picked up after a fumble.

Pootle
Usually on a bicycle, though often on foot. A leisurely meander around the back streets in the neighbourhood, often while partners are at a football match.

Tremble
A side effect from too many pub crawls.

Streak
Quickly over very short distances. Usually ends with a rugby tackle and a photograph posed in a policman's helmet. On no account confuse streaking with trambling.

Mumbles
Coastline in Wales.

Fumble
What tends to happen to teenagers in cars, or after goalkeepers mistakes (see Trundles below).

Scramble
Eggs on toast or Battle of Britain fighter pilots at dawn.

Trundle
Like a golf trolley on cobbles. Slow, dragging the feet, A teenager who missed out on the chance of a fumble, or football fans returning home after their team put up a good display but lost 1- 0 due to a mistake by the goal keeper.

t1 Portobello

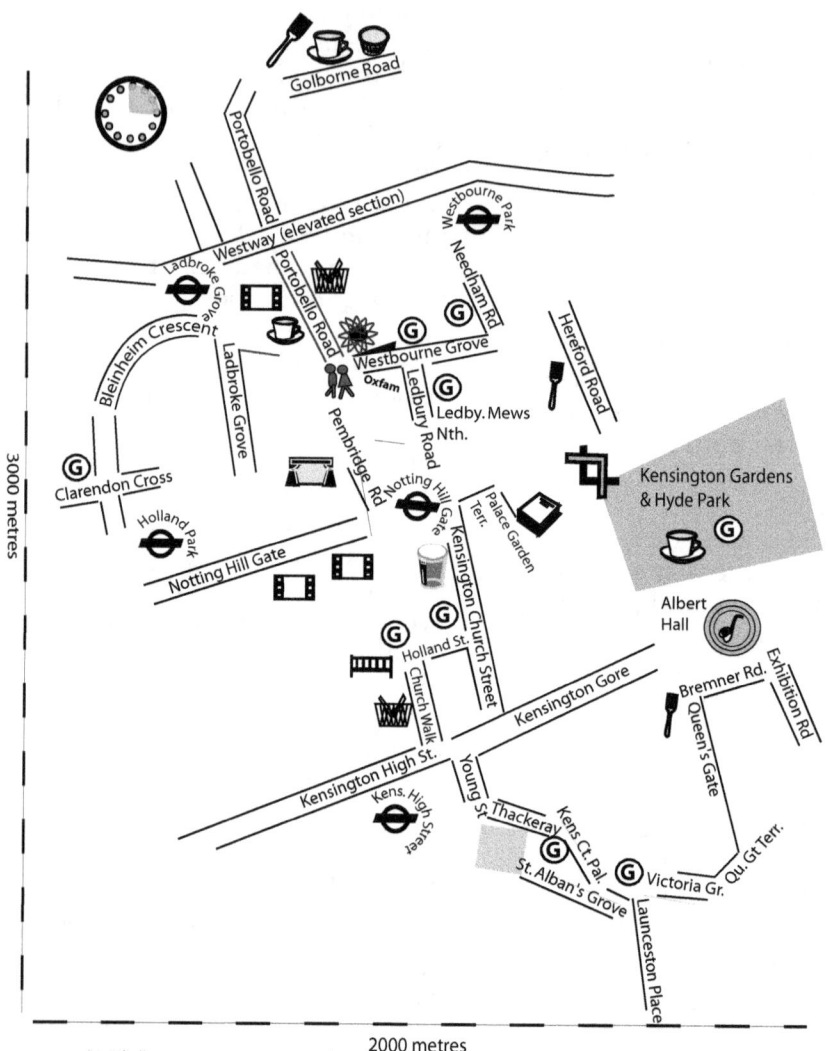

t1

Portobello, Notting Hill & Kensington

Let's start in the West. In the shadow of Trellick tower and the Westway. Vibrant bold colours, music in street markets, across Hyde Park into traditional mews and grand townhouses.

On **Golborne Road**

A mix of sweet Portuguese patisserie and Moroccan spice. One of the few remaining pie and mash shops stands as tribute to traditional English food.

Luxurious **Electric Cinema** with leather seats, footstools and screen bar so you can order drinks without missing the film.

Contrast Portobello with gentler Holland Park.
Turn right onto **Blenheim Crescent.** *Take a look* along *Clarendon Cross* before crossing back onto Ladbroke Grove.

Into **Westbourne Grove** a mix of fashionable old and new local in-dependent shops. Fashion, antiques, cafés and restaurants. Be prepared for crowds on weekends.

On *Westbourne Grove* **Oxfam** fashion store full to the brim with designer bargains.

Opposite a neat triangle with benches and florist **Wild at Heart.**

Our first gallery stop **England & Co.** A friendly contemporary art gallery. Paper sculptor Georgia Russell (see p.7)

www.englandgallery.com

About the Artist

Georgia Russell

Georgia Russell began creating paper sculpture while studying at the Royal College of Art.
Taking books, maps, music scores, and photographs which she manipulates re-constructs into extravagant, ornamental paper sculptures. It is immediately evident the sculptures take a great amount of care precision and patience. Work on educational projects and a sculptural installation at the Jubilee Library in Brighton. Her work has been exhibited in the V&A London, Paris Aberdeen, and recently USA

Georgia Russell creates paper sculpture by cutting and dissecting printed matter.

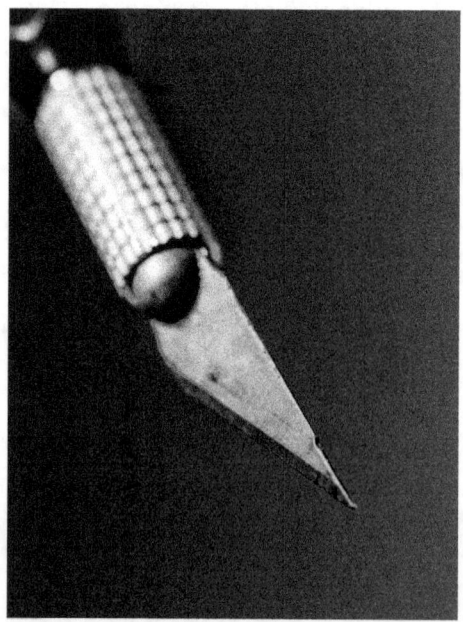

Further along **Ledbury Road**

Cosa discreetly tucked
inside **Ledbury Mews North.**

www.cosalondon.com

Back on **Westbourne Grove**
Turn right
Cross to **Needham Road**

Tiny **Flow** gallery
Ceramics, glass, paper, textiles, metal,
jewellery and contemporary crafts.

www.flowgallery.co.uk

Head up to *Notting Hill Gate*
via Pembridge Villas. Two more cinemas:

Coronet Cinema
www.coronet.org

Gate Picturehouse
www.picturehouses.co..uk

Plenty of bars, cafes and restaurants
to choose from along here.

A small independent bookshop
Notting Hill Books on **Palace Gardens**
(off Notting Hill Gate)
A tiny shop in the shadow of
hotels and offices selling out of print and
second hand books.
If you enjoy arts and antiques
head *up to* **Kensington Church Street**

t1 Notting Hill

On Kensington Church Street

The Churchill Arms
Recommended for good Thai food
in a traditional English pub.
Continue along *Kensington Church
Street* to **Holland Street**.
Richard Green's photography
gallery. Further along
Chanly, a family estate agents with
an art gallery inside.
Elephant & Castle pub opposite.

Kensington Church Walk
A pleasant detour along a narrow
lane. St. Mary Abbott's church, a
small garden with benches and a
row of shops.
Down to *Kensington High Street.*

From Notting Hill Gate
and Bayswater Road

On to **Hyde Park**
The statue *Physical Energy* by **George
Frederick Watts RA (1817-1904)**
The large bronze statue 'Physical Energy,' depicts a naked man on horse-
back, shielding his eyes from the sun
as he looks ahead of him.
*G.F.Watts was one of the most prolific
artists and contributors to art in the
19th century . Read more about Watt's
and Postman's Park on page 90*

In **Hyde Park**
The Serpentine Gallery

Exhibitions of a consistently high standard and a art bookshop.
Each summer a different architect is commissioned to build a spectacular summer pavilion in front of the gallery.

www.serpentinegallery.org

Leaving Hyde Park
Take time to view the reliefs on the **Royal Albert Hall**, and the beautiful ornate Royal College of Organists opposite.

From here you have a couple of options:

Return to Kensington Road, walk further down *Rutland Gate* and into *Knights-bridge* for *Beauchamp Place and Walton Street (see t2 Chelsea)*

Step down behind ***The Royal Albert Hall***
Head left and then turn right on to Exhibition Road
for **The Victoria and Albert Museum.**

Go right into **Bremner Street.**
Down to *Queen"s Gate Terrace.*
At the end of Queen's Gate *Terrace*
Cross Gloucester Road into Victoria Grove
Up to **Launceston Place**

Hackelbury Fine Arts
Specialising in 20th and 21st century fine
artand photography.
In 2005 I saw an inspirational exhibition
of black and white photographs of Japan
by Michael Kenna which demonstrated
to me the power of simplified
composition, that complements the
beautiful Japanese landscape
(more on p.14)

www.hackelbury.co.uk

After visiting *Hackelbury Fine Arts*
Round St. Alban's Grove
Up Kensington Court Road.
Left on to *Thackeray Street*

Gallery 19
Specialises in architectural art

www.gallery19.com

Mosaik
Interior decorator creating bespoke tile
patterns.

End this tramble in Kensington High Street

About the Artist

Michael Kenna

With night time exposures of up to ten hours, Michael Kenna's photographs often record details that the human eye is not able to perceive. These images, hand printed in black and white create an atmosphere of peace and stillness, inviting viewers to reflect and meditate upon them. Born in Widnes, England 1953, he currently lives in Seattle, Washington USA.

www.michaelkenna.com

A nocturnal photographer, working with long time-exposures who concentrates primarily on atmospheric conditions of the natural landscape.

t4 *Pimlico to Battersea*

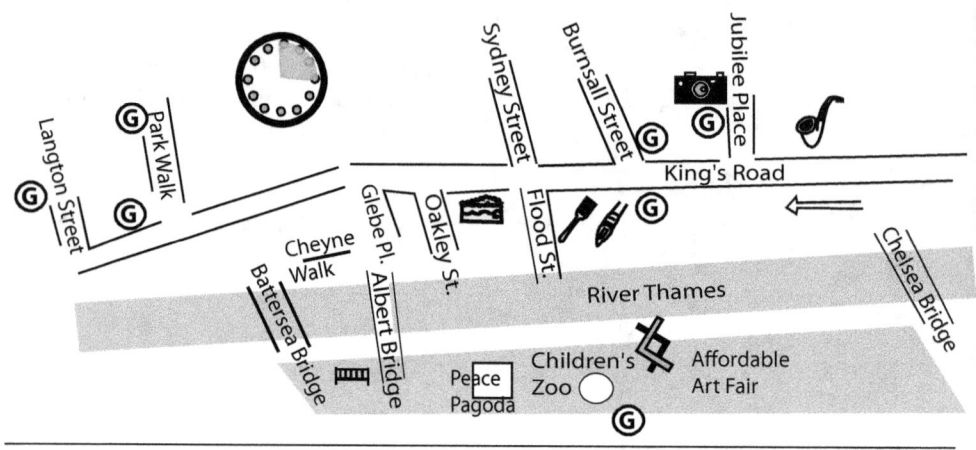

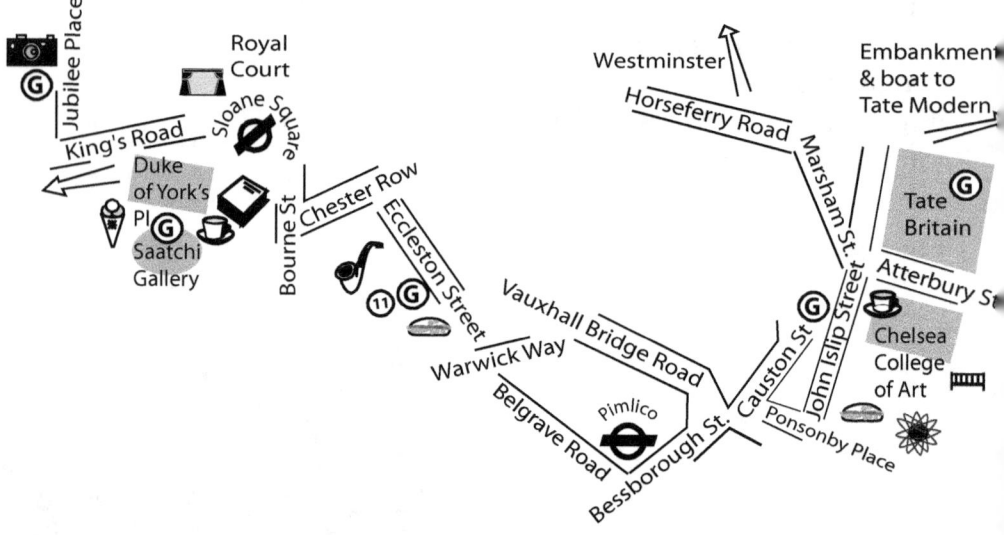

Pimlico, Belgravia Chelsea & Battersea

Long winding tramble that starts and ends by the River Thames. Around the leafy mews of Belgravia and ghosts of fashion past on King's Road. Cross the river on Albert Bridge for a picnic in Battersea Park next to the peace pagoda.

At **Pimlico** Station
Take the **Bessborough Road** *exit down to*
and across **Vauxhall Bridge Road**

The first gallery is **Long & Ryle**
on **John Islip Street.**

Manami Hayasaki exhibited here in 2009
(see p.18)

A little further along John Islip Street
the **Relish** sandwich shop.

Chelsea College of Art & Design

The **Chelsea Café**
Coffee at student rates, a bargain for
caffeine chasers. On bright sunny
mornings sit out in the square before
heading into **Tate Britain**

Enter **Tate Britain** *through the side*
entrance on **Atterbury Street.**
It's a quieter entrance and it brings you
straight to the heart of the galleries and
the cloakroom.
Allow 2-3 hours minimum to make a
comprehensive visit to *Tate Britain*

www.tate.org.uk

rn in Osaka, Japan. Lives and works in
ndon.

udied Japanese traditional painting in
oto City University of Arts, and finished
 fine art degree at Chelsea College of
t and Design in London.

yasaki studied traditional Japanese
honga painting, with dry pigments
ended in a glue solution, outlined using
ack ink. Then created her own
dividual expression in conceptual art
d presented life-sized artworks un-
nstrained by tradition and established
ncepts. Creating the outlines with a
alpel in black card.

yasaki's first solo exhibition in Japan
atured a series of garden-themed
orks

ww.manamihayasaki.com

About the Artist

Manami Hayasaki

Hayasaki works in black card with a scalpel. Inspired by the natural world, images represent human society, ego, or duality of life and death.

Heading away from *Tate Britain*
back the same way we arrived it is 3/4 mile
or 20 min walk up Vauxhall Bridge Road to
Eccleston Street in Victoria.
Chelsea's Sloane Square (see over) is about
40 mins on foot.

Crossing Victoria at **Warwick Way** *takes you to* **Eccleston Street**

Arrive at Victoria Coach Station around
lunchtime, make your way *to* **Capri Sandwich Bar** for ciabatta.

Cross **Buckingham Palace Road.**
We are now in Belgravia. Exclusive Italian
influenced Victorian houses, and private
mews.
Along **Eccleston Street**

Eleven
Contemporary art and photography.

www.elevenfineart.com

Next door the dark interior of the
Boisdale Jazz & Cigar Club
What a combination!

Joss Graham
Specialises in textiles from the Indian
subcontinent, sculpture, ceramics and
jewellery.

From **Eccleston Street**

It is a short 10 minute stroll to
Sloane Square *and the* **Kings Road.**

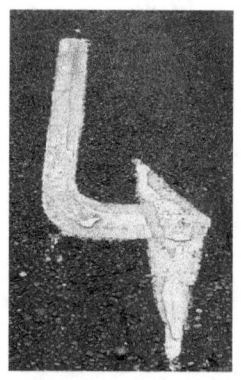

Option:
Leaving Tate Britain
Exit via the front entrance
Head to the Embankment to catch
the Tate boat across to Tate Modern
(see section t7 Waterloo)

London has an increasing number of urban squares and pedestrian spaces.

Just up from Sloane Square,

Duke of York's Place
Used to be an army barracks now an attractive square with cafés, fountains and benches. One of my favourite art bookshops **Taschen**
Excellent books, good value.

www.taschen.com/stores

Walking up from Sloane Square to Duke of York's Place.

'Two Pupils' by Allister Bowtell
A boy leapfrogs a post while a girl sits and watches him

On a sunny day, sit in Duke of York's Place enjoy an ice cream from the *Gelateria Valerie*
Watch the shoppers with their little dogs and bicycles on the King's Road.

The Saatchi Gallery

A grand white space. Contemporary art in 18 rooms over 3 floors Contemporary installations, sculpture and visual art from around the world. Saatchi continues to support and promote new British artists

www.saatchi-gallery.co.uk

The King's Road

You can sense the ghosts of fashion's past. Sixtie's glamour, a little Seventie's punk now faded beneath more conventional developments. It is still possible to find some eccentricities if you look closely along the sedate pastel homes.

Leaving The Saatchi Gallery behind you, walk up The King's Road past the exotic *Pizza Express (only in Chelsea!)*, colourful town houses and the Chelsea Potter pub.

Reach Jubilee Place

Michael Hoppen Gallery

Devoted to photography by established and emerging artists. Continuous display of vintage collectible photographs, while promoting new photographers.

www.michaelhoppengallery.com

Choose to:
Head North across **Elyston Place.**

Walk up **Elyston Street.**
Turn right on to **Brompton Road** for the decorative coloured tiles and stained glass *Bibendum* building.

Cross **Brompton Road** on to **Pelham Street** which leads to South Kensington
Or
Turn right at **Brompton Road** on to **Walton Street** for **Coskun** and **Walton Fine Art.**

From **Jubilee Place** walk towards the quieter end of the *King's Road.*

Tucked in the courtyard in **Burnsall Street** tiny **Flying Colours** gallery

www.flyingcoloursgallery.com

Colourful Ad Hoc.
Formerly *Boy*, the glam punk's honeypot.

Chelsea Cinema
Part of the *Curzon* group of cinemas
(see also t5 Bloomsbury, and t6 Mayfair)

Pass the clock at Chelsea Town Hall.
Confetti at Chelsea Registry office.
Decorative plaques and tiles on the
King's Road.

Up to Glebe Place

Ealing Studio's film director Carol Reed
whose films included The Stars Look
Down, The Third Man, and Oliver! Lived
at 213 along this stretch of the King's
Road
The sculptor William McMillan (see p.24)
lived in Glebe Place.
Also admire glamorous art nouveau
architecture at no.50 During the nine-
teenth century many artists studios
around here and down on Cheyne Walk
alongside the River Thames.

About the Artist

William McMillan
(1887 - 1977)

Trained as a sculptor at Gray's School of Art in Aberdeen, and then the Royal College of Art from 1908 to 1912. In the 1914-1919 war he served in the 5th Oxfordshire and Buckinghamshire Light Infantry. Survived winter 1915-16 in Ypres.

After the war his reputation grew and by 1925 he was elected an associate of the Royal Academy. He became a Royal Academician in 1933.

Sadly an assault and robbery in the street left him badly injured. McMillan died in hospital just after his 90th birthday.

McMillan's work included:
Bust of Admiral Beatty and fountain bronzes in Trafalgar Square
A sculpture of Lord Trenchard stands in Victoria Embankment Gardens.
A Statue of George VI overlooking The Mall
Statue of Alcock and Brown outside the old visitor's centre at Heathrow.
Statue of Turner in the staircase of the Royal Academy.

24

I have been visiting Stockpot in the
King's Road on and off for over twenty
years. It is good value, with friendly
speedy service.

Art supplies
Green and Stone at no.259

Extend your tramble to the top end
of the King's Road.
Take in some of the architecture, and
more traditional shops at World's End.

Kings Road Gallery at 436

Further along King's Road on Park Walk

Jonathan Cooper
www.jonathancooper.co.uk

Langton Street Gallery
www.9langtonstreet.co.uk

Battersea Park

Stroll alongside the *Thames at sunrise or sunset.*

In Spring and Autumn there is an excellent ***Affordable Art Fair*** with a courtesy bus from Sloane Square. Art available from around £50.

From **Chelsea Bridge**

Pump House Gallery

A public art space promoting work by emerging artists from Wandsworth

Childrens Zoo

With otters and inside the meerkat enclosure a ground level dome where children can go face to face with meerkats

The golden Peace Pagoda sparkling in the sun.

On to Albert Bridge. The most decorative and delicate pastel pink and blue covered in tiny lights, Extend your tramble to the more sedate but equally elegant Battersea Bridge Take time to admire the detailed ornamental ironwork of both bridges.

Battersea
Peace
Pagoda .
Built
by Buddhist
Monks and Nuns.

Dedicated to
the realisation
of Universal peace.

Each day a chance
To discover streets
Escape through an alley
Into a room to dream.

Commuters dance
around the station
Navigate escalators
ticket hall exit fast

Elbows out, firmly advance
No room for hesitation
Keep left, Stay right
Cut across the stream

Patience rewards prospectors
Stillness slowly paces
around spectators
the city breathes at last

**Fitzroy Square
and it's surrounds.**

The narrow stretch between
Marylebone and Bloomsbury
from Oxford Street to Euston Road
Between **Great Portland Street**
and **Gower Street**
Best known for housing London's
publishers, advertising agencies
and production companies.

A rich seam for art galleries.

Named after the land owned
by Charles Fitzroy who
commissioned Robert Adam
to design Fitzroy Square in 1790.

A favourite area for Bohemian
artists and writers that
included George Bernard Shaw,
and Virginia Woolf.

Fitzrovia

**At the start
of the
Twentieth Century
the centre
of
Bohemian
London**

Fitzrovia t3

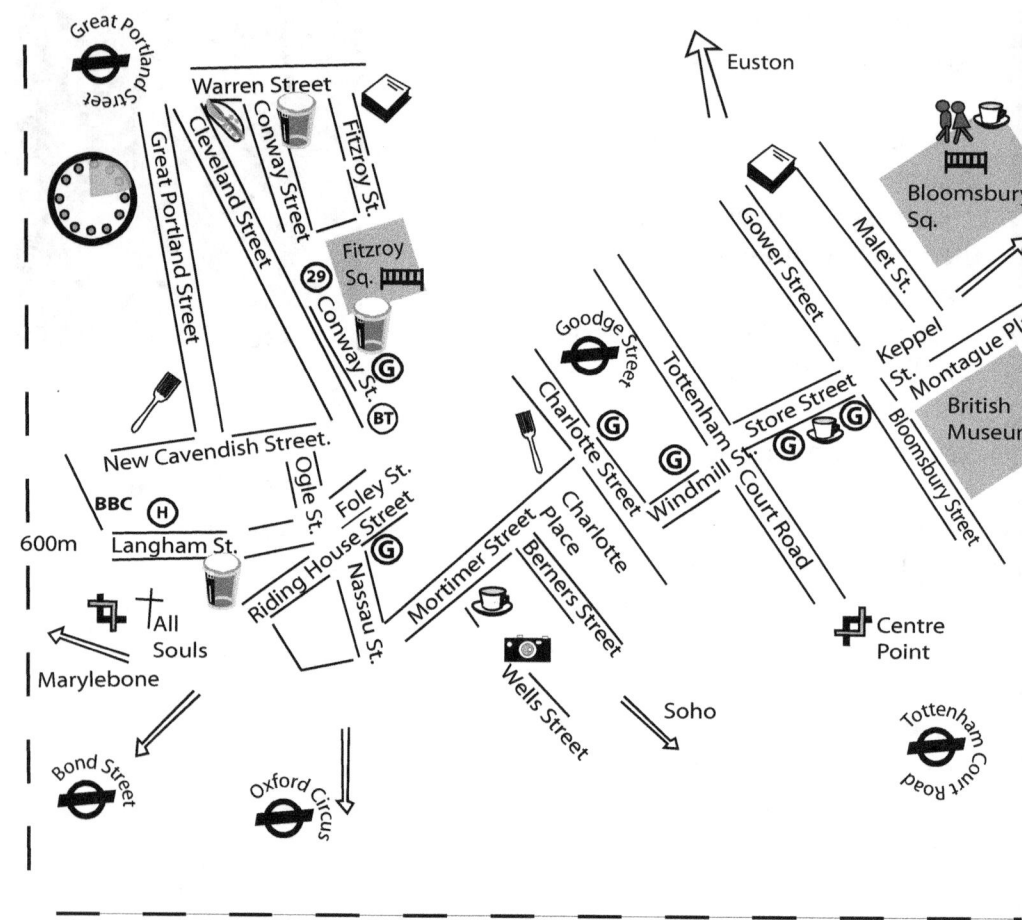

Exit **Great Portland Street**
tube station, quieter, more interesting
architecture than Euston Square.

Head along **Warren Street**

J.Evans once a dairy, now a deli,
smart decorative gold and blue tiled
front.

The Smuggler's Tavern with it's
heroic figurehead raises a smile.

Fitzroy Street

Samuel French's Theatre Bookshop
has been selling theatrical
history books, scripts, programmes,
since 1830.

Fitzroy Square

Designed by Robert Adams in the 1790s.
The square was completed in the 1830s.
Embassy flags flutter freely alongside
elegant Georgian houses. No. 29 the
home of and George Bernard Shaw. and
later Virginia Woolf,
The square is also home of the Jerwood
Fund, which supports the arts.

For Jerwood Space
see p77 t7 Waterloo - Bankside

About the Artist

Naomi Blake

Born in Czechoslovakia Naomi Blake survived childhood spent in Auschwitz. Studied at Hornsey School of Art in North London, and has been exhibiting sculpture across the UK since 1962.

Her work has been exhibited in many galleries around the world. Find out more about Naomi Blake's work by visiting the Curwen Gallery *(see page 36)*

View by Naomi Blake in Fitzroy Square

On Conway Street you can see the base of the **BT tower.**

Rebecca Hossack

(see Charlotte Street over also)

Rebecca Hossack was born in Melbourne in 1955. According to the website, Rebecca came to England in the early eighties to study law at Lincoln's Inn, but switched to her own art business. Just shows with the right intentions it can be hugely successful to change careers!

www.r-h-g.co.uk

Next to the gallery is *the* **Lukin** *pub.* Enjoy reasonably priced bangers and mash, and steak pies.

This is a good example of trambling. A mix of great architecture, tea, and galleries no urgency, but with intention to discover more art and new parts of London.

Walk round onto **Cleveland Street.** The distinctive profile of the *BT Tower* which is still affectionately referred to as the Post Office tower and can be seen for miles around. Take a minute to see the entrance, and the steel architecture at the base. It's good to know where the roots lie!

Cross onto **New Cavendish Street**

Down Ogle Street, to **Foley Street,** and into **Langham Street**, the *Yorkshire Grey pub* has a smart fascia, and Samuel Smith ales.

Opposite the *Yorkshire Grey* is the smart chequerboard pattern of the Langham Court Hotel

Further along *Langham Street* - Seafood and Italian restaurants.

Cut through Candover Street on to Riding House Street

Look up at the gold and green tiled mosaics signs on the sides of mansion blocks.
Turn right down *Nassau Street* on to **Mortimer Street**

Time for lunch!
Great Titchfield Street
Scandinavian Kitchen

I have mentioned a few favourites in each section. You may prefer to use your time exploring, take your lunch with you, rather than stopping.

Make time for tea and cake!

*Trambling is inexpensive
and can be enjoyed on little money
Once you are in the
centre of London, you just
need a little money
for refreshments.*

Mortimer Street

At the heart of London's fashion & film production business. If you have been shopping in Oxford Circus it is worth escaping here for welcome relief from the crowds.

Ligne Roset

International modern lighting and furniture store established in 1930

Café Teo is good value for the West End.

From **Mortimer Street** you can either choose **Berners Street** into the heart of *Soho* or up to **Charlotte Street.**

Top of *Mortimer Street*
close to *Upper Regent Stree*t

Into **Charlotte Street**

Rebecca Hossack Gallery
(see also Conway Street on p32)
Australian Aboriginal art

On **Tottenham Street**

The Coningsby Gallery
Contemporary Illustrators

www.coningsbygallery.com

*Some unusual murals around
Pollock's, a curious toy museum.*

An important feature on **Windmill Street**

Curwen Gallery

Established for more than 50 years. Representing a wide range of artists, and specialist limited edition print makers. The gallery on two floors is a great way to get to know variety of artists and art styles.

www.curwengallery.co.uk

See also *The Rectory* in *Spitalfields* **t8**

Once you have visited Curwen Gallery, you may be inspired to learn more about printmaking. **Curwen** have a print study centre teaching traditional and contemporary printmaking skills to artists, schools, students and teachers.

www.curwenprintstudy.co.uk

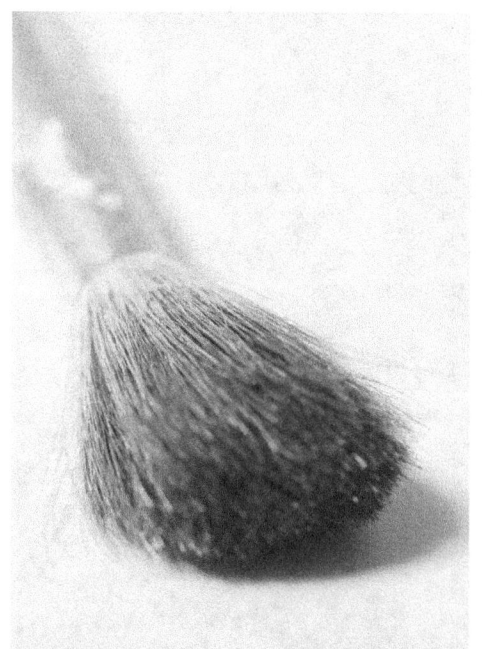

At the end of Windmill Street
Cross Tottenham Court Road
On *Store Street*

The Building Centre

Informative display of new buildings
and developments in London.
All based on a model to give a good
sense of the changing face of city.
An excellent bookshop for architect's
reference and building design, small
café.

www.buildingcentre.co.uk

Stay on Store Street.
Further along on the right hand side
The Political Cartoon Gallery.
Satirical cartoons and caricatures from
the start of the last century including
current day genius of Steve Bell and
Martin Rowson.
Exit Store Street on to *Keppel Street* into
Montague Place brings you to the
British Museum.

*Continue this tramble in Bloomsbury t4 p.38
over*

Amazing Glaze

Once a practical decorative addition to shop fronts, pubs and entrances. Excellent examples of tiled fascias can still be found across London and are shown elsewhere in this guide. Many shops and pubs have been converted to other uses. As high streets fill with temporary plastic fascias, the permanence of tiles is a reminder of the craftsmanship and quality of days gone by. Beautiful colours catching the morning sunlight.

Still a key feature in tube stations. A few survivors spotted on trambles pictured below.

More tiles please!

Bloomsbury

t4

Bloomsbury tramble sounds like it has taken it's name from a dessert menu. *Perfect in autumn* when summer crowds have left the British Museum. *Head for the October Gallery.*

Statue of Mahatma Ghandi by Fredda Brilliant, in Tavistock Square
(See profile p.42)

Bloomsbury t

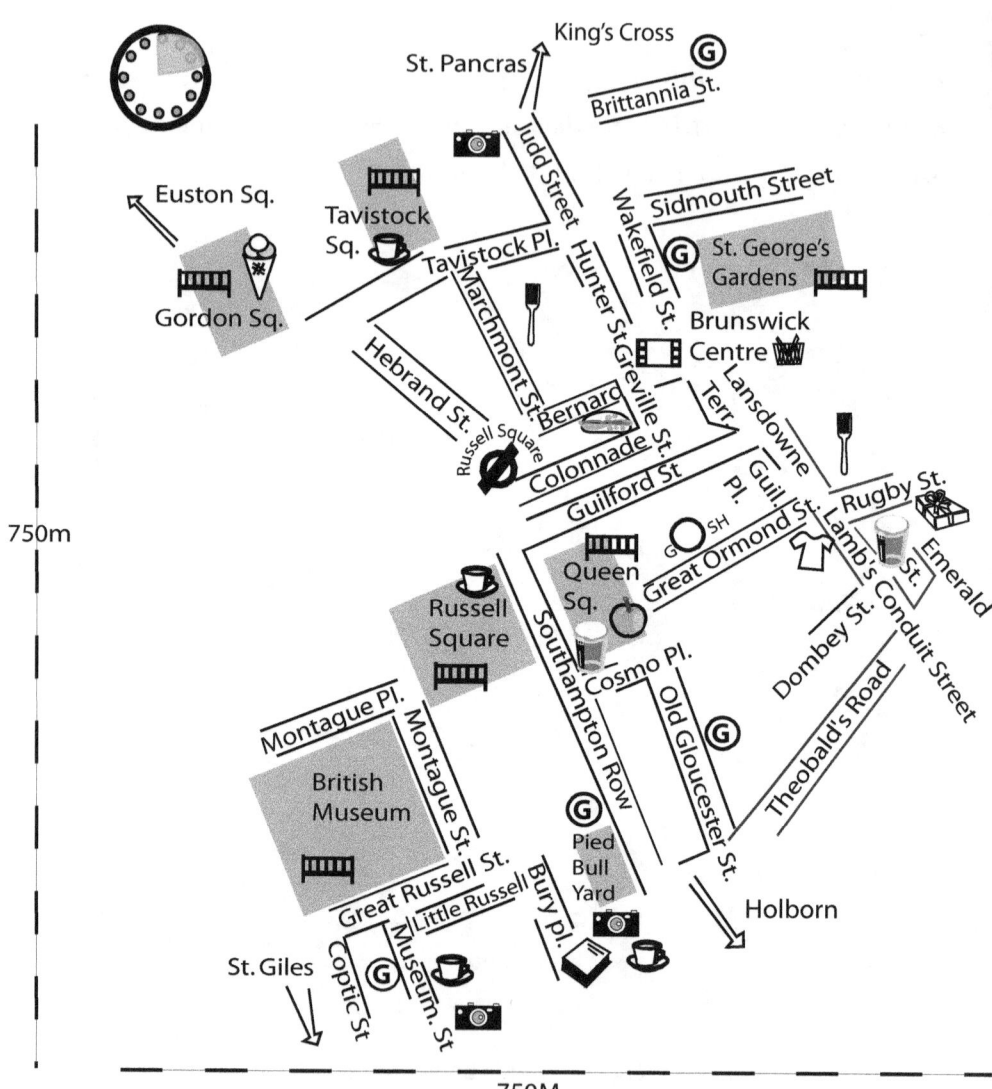

King's Cross

St. Pancras

Brittannia St.

Euston Sq.

Tavistock Sq.

Gordon Sq.

Tavistock Pl.

Judd Street

Hunter St.

Wakefield St.

Sidmouth Street

St. George's Gardens

Brunswick Centre

Marchmont St.

Hebrand St.

Greville St.

Bernard

Russell Square

Colonnade

Lansdowne Terr.

Guilford St.

Guilford Pl.

Great Ormond St.

Lamb's Conduit Street

Rugby St.

Emerald St.

750m

Montague Pl.

Montague St.

British Museum

Russell Square

Queen Sq.

Southampton Row

Cosmo Pl.

Old Gloucester St.

Dombey St.

Theobald's Road

Holborn

St. Giles

Coptic St.

Museum. St.

Great Russell St.

Little Russell

Bury Pl.

Pied Bull Yard

750M

If you choose to visit **The British Museum,** enter from **Montague Place**. It's quicker to get to the exhibits, a lot simpler and less crowded than the front entrance in *Great Russell Street.*

Extended Tramble
From Russell Square
to King's Cross.

Start in **Tavistock Garden**
The memorial to Mahatma Gandhi
Sculpture by **Fredda Brilliant**

Walk up **Tavistock Street**
to *Judd Street* and **Wakefield Street Dairy** *an occasional exhibition space.* A little tricky to spot, it is on the corner set back from the road.

Continue to **Russell Square**

About the Artist

Fredda Brilliant
(1903 –1999)

Among others to sit for her was Indira Gandhi. Brilliant created "The Eyes of India" only half a face is shown, forcing the viewer to concentrate on the eyes; Brilliant made busts in 1948 and 1951 of Nehru in India. Ants destroyed one bust, and intense heat desiccated another. As well as working as a sculptor, Brilliant wrote a novel, a series of interviews with political leaders, and a selection of stories. Brilliant was a fellow of the Royal Society of Arts and a member of the Society of Portrait Sculptors. She died in Illinois USA May 1999.

Born Lodz, Poland.
Travelled and worked across the world. This statue of Mahatma Ghandi was unveiled by Harold Wilson, then Prime Minister, in 1965.

From *Russell Square Gardens*

Head on to **Guilford Street** and down the cobbled mews of ***The Colonnade.*** Invariably back streets such as *this one* are empty in the middle of the day, a welcome relief from the noise of *Woburn Place* and other busy thoroughfares in the area.

Leaving The Colonnade
Café Romano another fine example of the many family run cafés in London.

44

Up **Greville Street**

Enter **The Brunswick Centre**

Renoir Cinema
Another of the Curzon cinema chain (*see t6 Mayfair*). Small and comfortable with a bar. Good selection of European and World cinema.

www.curzoncinemas.com/venues/renoir_cinema/

Behind Great Ormond Street
Hospital

Lamb's Conduit Street

Perseverence Pub & Dining Room
Steak pies, sausage and mash.

Folk Clothing
Functional and stylish.
Another perfect trambler's
store!
www.folkclothing.com

Cigala
Spanish Tapas restaurant
www.cigala.co.uk

Langham Street Gallery

Contemporary paintings including Karl
Davies, Michael Kidd, Vincent Barquez,

www.langhamgallery.com

Rugby Street

Art Deco jewellery & Gifts **French's Dairy**
a good example of a traditional tiled
fascia preserved and still in use.
When I visited *Rugby Street three shops,*
Sussanh Hunter, Ben Pentreath and
French's Dairy had installed flags above
their shops, I thought it added an extra
touch of theatre to the street.
I hope they are still flying in future.

www.susannahhunter.com
www.benpentreath.com
www.frenchsdairy.com

46

Back on Great Ormond Street
Head for **Queen's Square**
and St. George's Garden

On to **Old Gloucester Street**

The October Gallery

Housed inside a Victorian girls school
built in 1863.
Opened in 1979 displaying
contemporary art from all cultures,
specialising in African artists.
As well as exhibition space, there is a
courtyard, cafe, theatre space, and club
room available for hire

www.octobergallery.co.uk

Through **Cosmo Place**
to *Southampton Row* towards *Holborn* or
Russell Square Gardens.

Return to **Judd Street**

Photo Books

Specialist photographic book store.
A fabulous range of out of print and
secondhand books and great value.

Exit Judd Street onto Euston Road
by **The British Library**

If you can bear crowds of commuters
visit **St Pancras Station**

At the top of the stairs a statue
 in honour of *Sir John Betjeman*
by *Martin Jennings (see over)*
Beneath the station clock
The Meeting Place by *Paul Day*
(more over)

British artist specialising in figurative art, Paul Day trained at Colchester, Dartington, and Cheltenham. Creates engaging panoramic relief sculptures in terracotta, resin, and bronze.

A nine metre high statue of a couple embracing stands beneath the station clock. *'The Meeting Place'* commissioned for St. Pancras Station.

Other commissions undertaken by the artist include The Battle of Britain Memorial in Westminster, Queen Mother Memorial in the Mall, Urban Comedy in Brussels.

www.pauldaysculpture.com

About the Artist

Paul Day

About the Artist

Martin Jennings

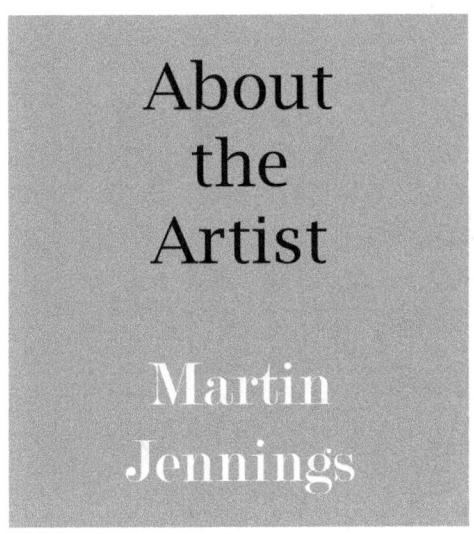

Leave The Betjeman Arms
*Up **York Way*** Approximately 200 metres to **King's Place**

Two galleries, one right at the front of the building, the second is downstairs toward the back of the building. Frequent concerts at lunchtime and early evening.

Step out to the canal and a fine display of barges part of the **Canal Museum.**

A commission to create a bronze of Sir Edward Heath led to requests for busts of entrepreneurs and industrialists. Jennings was selected by St. Paul's Cathedral in London to make a bust of H.M. Queen Elizabeth the Queen Mother to celebrate her 100th birthday.

Sir John Betjeman *(1906 -1984)*
Poet, writer and broadcaster,
Born in Hampstead Poet Laureate
in 1972, championed and fought
to save Victorian architecture including
St Pancras station. Saved it from
demolition to be restored and re-opened
in 2006.
The Betjeman Arms
All day menu Full English breakfast, beer battered fish & chips, pies and puddings. The specially brewed Betjeman ale, plus guest beers.

St. Giles t5

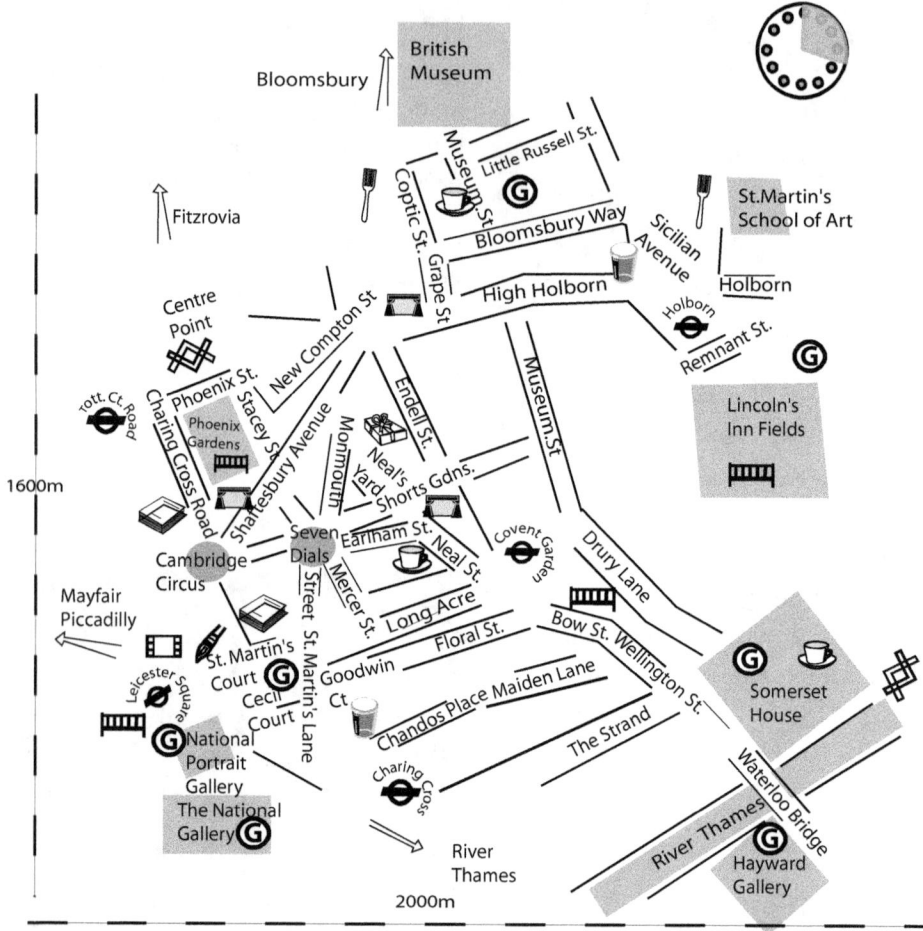

St. Giles, Seven Dials & The Strand

ramble through the heart of Theatreland.

ariety, colour, romantic escapism.
nter from Cambridge Circus, through Seven Dials.
aking in collector's shops, *you may spot actors arriving* at theatre stage doors.
nticipate a chance meeting in a hotel doorway.

here is a joyous atmosphere, *laughter rings out, celebration is in the air*
s crowds surround street entertainers.

ross Covent Garden to Somerset House on The Strand.

xtend across the Thames at Waterloo B ridge to The Hayward Gallery.

t5 St. Giles

Start in front of the British *Museum* on **Great Russell Street**
Into **Bury Place** and **Pied Bull Yard** including Leica specialist camera shop.

London Review of Books
One of London's leading independent bookstores with a small café inside.

www.lrbshop.co.uk

Austin Desmond Fine Art
*Specialist i*n Modern British paintings, sculptures and ceramics.

www.austindesmond.com

There are more quirky shops here. **Blade** stamp shop make stamps to order.

Head onto **Gilbert St**

Down **Little Russell Street**
Cross **Museum Street**

Camera Café
for collectible cameras.

Into **Coptic Street**

Take a moment to admire the *art nouveau* building on the corner. Built in 1888. Once a dairy supplies company. After the successful opening of the first *Pizza Express in Wardour Street in 1965,* .artist Enzo Apicella was commissioned to design the interior of the next restaurant in the chain which opened in 1967.

Cross **Bloomsbury Way** *and New Oxford Street*

James Smith & Sons
Umbrella business established in 1830, moved to it's current site in 1857. The Victorian shop front remains virtually unaltered for 150 years. Continues to make. traditional umbrellas and walking sticks in the basement

Diagonal on **Grape Street** brings you out neatly between the stage door to the **Shaftesbury Theatre** and the **Cuban Embassy.** A juxtaposition that you could really only expect to see in London. The Cuban flag greets you as you exit Grape Street.

Cross High Holborn
South on to **Endell Street**
or
Head West on Shaftesbury Avenue towards Cambridge Circus

Phoenix Garden

Cross Shaftesbury Avenue behind the
Phoenix Theatre. *Off New Compton Street*
A community garden that must be
praised for creativity and inventiveness
Benches to sit at, read, and eat lunch
.

Leave Phoenix Gardens round *Flitcroft
Street* at the side of the *Phoenix Theatre.*

On to **Charing Cross Road**

Plenty of bookshops and ***Ray's Jazz***
inside **Foyle's** bookshop.
The cafe on the first floor is a good
vantage point to people watch from.

Seven Dials

Four streets meet and lead in seven directions to Covent Garden and surrounding theatres.

At the centre are sun dials.
On one corner is a graph with calculations on how to read the time throughout the year. However you may find it much simpler to check your watch!

More than I can possibly describe on a couple of pages. The secret of Seven Dials is to trip through the corners and alley ways, and find your favourites.

Monmouth Street
Covent Garden Hotel
Monmouth Coffee Bar
Pop Boutique
Orla Keily Shop

Shorts Gardens
Neal's Yard

Earlham Street
The Donmar Warehouse Theatre
Magma Comic bookstore

From **Mercer Street**
Go on to Long Acre, and down Bow Street or Drury Lane to reach Somerset House on the Strand.

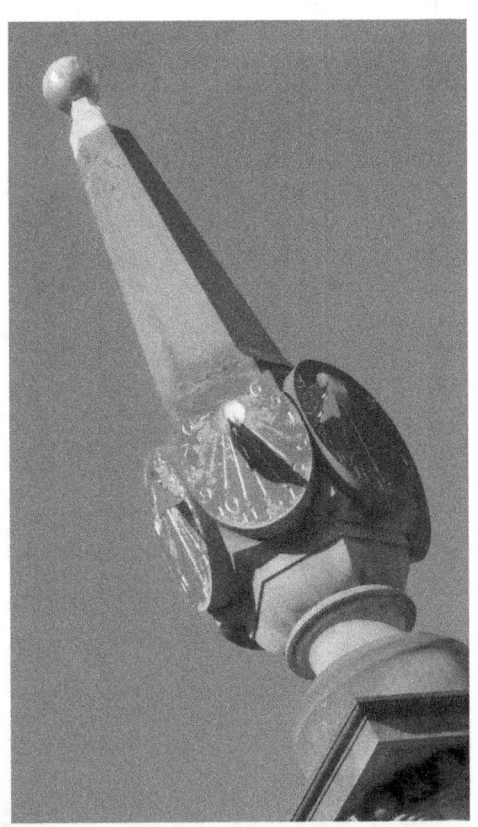

Around **St. Martin's Lane**

St. Martin's Court *and* **Cecil Court** with antique and collectors shops in between theatres stage doors.

Tenderpixel Gallery
Small space dedicated to art technology and media.

Across opposite, narrow **Goodwin Court** leads up to *Covent Garden*

Alternatively continue down *St. Martin's Lane* to **The National Gallery** or on to The Strand and ***Somerset House.***

Back on Charing Cross Road. Head to **Cass Arts** Always good value. *Time to stock up!*

The National Portrait Gallery

In addition to the major collection of paintings, the best gallery in London to promote photography as a major art form. Consistently good displays Drop in to see the latest acquisitions major shows. or immerse yourself in the collection for a couple of hours. Great view over London from the cafe on the 5th floor.

www.npg.org.uk

To get to Somerset House from the National Portrait Gallery walk up Chandos Place, Maiden Lane, past the birth place of JMW Turner and past Rules the oldest restaurant in London opened in 1798, down on to The Strand.

Somerset House

Standing on the site of a Tudor palace that was demolished in 1775.
Inside **The Courtauld Institute** a fine display of Impressionist paintings on four floors. Entrance to the gallery is currently free before 2pm on Monday. The courtyard plays host to open air films concerts and events throughout summer. With fountains, and an ice rink in winter. Embankment galleries, with frequent exhibitions, and talks. Café and restaurant overlooking the River Thames.

www.somersethouseprints.com

Waterloo Bridge
& The Hayward Gallery

Ahead of the *t7* tramble around *Waterloo* to *Tate Modern* on *page 72,* It is worth taking a preview and a refreshing walk across *Waterloo Bridge.*

Magnificent views up and down river. A good perspective on how the river winds through the city with views down on to the *Southbank.*
Once you reach the *Hayward Gallery* go up to the viewing space and look back across the river from South to North. Particularly rewarding at sunset.

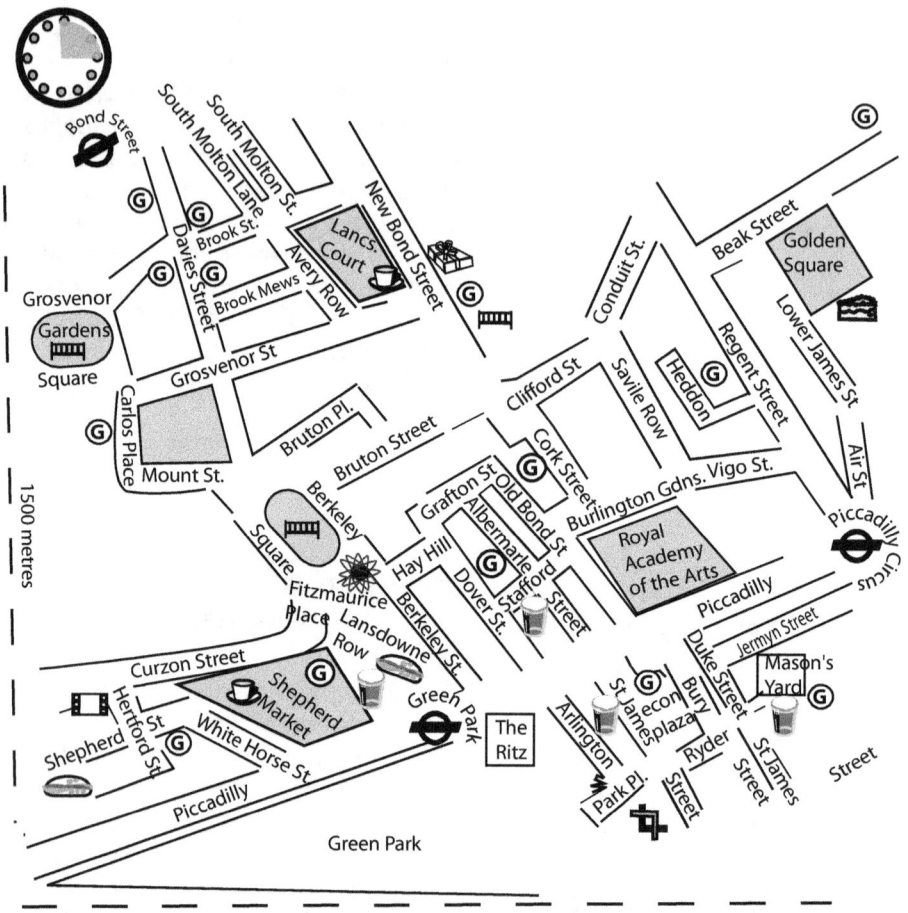

1500 metres

Mayfair, St. James's & Piccadilly

Easy tramble between *art dealers and London's most exclusive addresses. Start* at Green Park Station on Piccadilly.

The Royal Academy

Get to **The Royal Academy** ahead of opening time at 10a.m.
Especially if you are visit the popular Summer Exhibition between June and August.
Allow around two hours to view the displays.

If you don't have time to see the Royal Academy on this visit,
take a moment to admire the display in the courtyard entrance.

www.royalacademy.org.uk

t6 Mayfair

Leaving **The Royal Academy**

Cross **Piccadilly**
on to *Duke Street St. James's* between the colourful *Fortnum & Mason* windows and the elegant *Dunhill* building.

Take a look down Jermyn Street
Gentleman's outfitters, try not to be distracted by shoes shirts and suits. Unless you really can afford it!

The handsome **Swaine Adeney Brigg** store can be seen on the corner of *St. James's Street* (at the end of Jermyn Street). Luxury leather goods, and a fine collection of trambling essentials including walking sticks, canes, and umbrellas.

From Duke Street into **Mason's Yard** *Discreetly tucked away,* you may have passed by on previous occasions.
Enter at the side of **Chequer's Inn**
Nip in for a quick half of London Pride, early lunchtime.

White Cube
Standing proud in the centre of *Mason's Yard*

www.whitecube.com
also in Hoxton see t8

Just down from *Mason's Yard*
Around the corner in **Ryder Street**
Chris Beetle's Gallery
Specialist in watercolours, oils, illustrations, cartoons, & photographs.

www.chrisbeetles.com

Reach the end of Ryder Street cross over to **Bury Street**

Sims Reed Gallery at the base of the *Economist* Building, *then step up over Economist Plaza to* frequently changing art displays.

Cross into **Park Place** up the stairs tucked on the corner.
Up the steps to **Arlington Street** and the *Blue Posts* pub taking time to admire the selection of limousines waiting outside *The Ritz*.

Just opposite The Ritz
The Wolseley restaurant housed in grade II listed 160 Piccadilly. Famous for it's grill. Go for breakfast from 7am. Open until midnight.

www.thewolseley.com

Cross Piccadilly
Go straight up *Dover Street Galleries Galore! (skip to page 67)* or turn left into *Shepherd Market*

Shepherd Market

Turn left down Piccadilly approx.100yds
turn right into Shepherd Market via
White Horse Street. A fine collection
of pubs, cafés, ideal tramble territory.

Caffé Inn with walls covered
in photographs..

Panter & Hall
Specialists in 20th Century Scottish and
Contemporary British Art.

www.panterandhall.com

One favourite of mine is the tiny
Piccolo Sandwich bar in *Shepherd Street*.
Popular with London cabbies which is
always a good indicator!

Check the film screening times at nearby
Curzon Cinema in *CurzonStreet*.

www.curzoncinemas.com

If you don't fancy a film continue on
Curzon Street past the grand *Saudi Arabian* embassy..

Curzon Street brings you out on to *Berkeley Square*. An opportunity to sit and
plan the rest of your tramble.

Around **Berkeley Square**

Lansdowne House & The Lansdowne Club

Designed by Robert Adams in 1763 In 1782 Prime Minister Lord Shelburne, conceded independence to the United States. The Treaty of Paris, drawn up with Benjamin Franklin in the Round Room. Between 1921-1929 the house was leased to Gordon Selfridge, department store owner.

Continue straight through to **Lancaster Row**. Plenty of cheap eats and a popular flower stall.

Up **Hay Hill** to the centre of the West End Art Dealer's domain.

Alternatively, cross Berkeley Square, and head to Carlos Place (go to p.70)

Lorenzo Quinn

Sculptor Lorenzo Quinn, son of actor Anthony Quinn. commissioned by the United Nations in New York at just 21 years of age. Quinn has exhibited around the world,

The sculpture Give & Take III by Lorenzo Quinn in Berkeley Square.

Galleries galore!

Behind the Royal Academy. Take plenty of time to explore the wide variety of galleries.

On **Albemarle Street**

Brown's Hotel

Celebrated English hotel. The first to open in London in 1837

Upstairs at **The King's Head**

Traditional pub food.

John Martin Gallery

Represent a fine selection of contemporary artists. Recent exhibitions including Barry McGlashan and Andrew Gifford

www.jmlondon.com

Further down from *the King's Head* back towards *Piccadilly* **Carpenter's Workshop** Gallery and **Albemarle** Gallery.

Cork Street

Wide choice of galleries to please all art
lovers. Favourites include:

Beaux Arts
Exhibiting Modern British and contemporary sculptors and painters.

www.beauxartslondon.co.uk

Flowers
With a growing collection of
contemporary photography.
(see also Flowers East – t9 East p.98)

www.flowerseast.com

Bernard Jacobson

A neat tardis-like space that
appears to extend as you walk through.

www.jacobsongallery.com

Swan along **Savile Row**

Hauser & Wirth
(also in Piccadilly)
Major space for sculpture
and contemporary art.

If you can afford it go ahead and get
measured up for the best in British tailor-
ing, otherwise just pretend and window
shop like I do! The more colourful tailor's
windows are almost like galleries.
My favourite is *Ozwald Boateng*. I like the
look of the store, even though I may not
be able to afford the suits.

www.ozwaldboateng.co.uk

At no.5 *Look down* for the discreet
basement entrance to **James Hyman
Gallery** Photography and Modern
British art.

www.jameshymangallery.com

Once in *Savile Row* it is worth
extending your tramble along *VIgo Street*
back on to *Regent Street* into *Heddon
Street*.

Aicon Gallery

www.aicongallery.com

On the corner of **Carlos Place** is a
fountain with the statue of a nymph by
Greco

At no.15 **Timothy Taylor**

Recently showed Diane Arbus, Sean
Scully Craigie Aitchison, Bridget Riley,
Agnes Martin

www.timothytaylorgallery.com

Next door at no.13
Hamilton's Gallery

A leading photographic gallery. In the
past I have seen shows by Linda
McCartney, and more recently Irving
Penn. Good print collection

www.hamiltonsgallery.com

Walk around Carlos Place into
Grosvenor Square

Cross on to *Davies Street (see following
page)* for **Gagosian Gallery**

At the end of Cork Street
Turn left into *Clifford Street,*

Right on to **New Bond Street**
Chauffeurs sit in attendance outside many of the exclusive boutiques. Good for car spotters.

Bench!"Allies"
Sculpture of Churchill and Roosevelt in friendly discussion, by the american artist **Lawrence Holofcener**. A prolific poet, playwright, novelist, actor, director and sculptor. Holofcener has performed on stage and television, as well as writing and creating many works of art. installed in 1995 to commemorate 50 years since the end of World War II.

www.holofcener.com

More benches on street corners please!

Another favourite on *New Bond Street*
Fine Arts Society.

Elegant displays of 19th and 20th Century art and furniture. Founded in 1876. The gallery shows work by contemporary artists. Downstairs modern white space is a stark contrast to the traditional decor of upper floors.

www.faslondon.com

Halcyon
A modern art space housed in an elegant five-storey Georgian building. Worth a visit to view the staircase alone!

www.halcyongallery.com

Halcyon have a second gallery on Bruton Street, which leads to Berkeley Square.

Further up New Bond Street
Take a diversion into *Lancashire Court.*
A charming mews with café, restaurants
and a spa.

www.lancashirecourt.com

Exit into Brook Street or take the diagonal
up Avery Row.
Stop off at *Paul Smith sales shop,* see if
you can find a bargain.

At no 23 and 25 **Brook Street**

Handel Museum

The site where Handel and Jimi Hendrix
were neighbours approx. 200 years apart.
Now the Handel museum .

www.handelhouse.org

South Molton Lane

When *South Molton Street* is busy
I like to walk on *South Molton Lane*
by the auction halls. Look out for events,
exhibitions, and sample sales at The
Music Room

www.themusicroom.co.uk

This flexible space has meeting rooms
and a theatre space. *Margaret Howell*
hold a sample sale here. Simple, elegant
men's and women's clothing *Ideal for
trambles!*

www.margarethowell.co.uk

Davies Street

Gagosian Gallery
Small display.
Larger gallery in Britannia Street King's
Cross, (either extend from **t4** p.30, or start
of **t11** p115)

www.gagosian.com

Gimpel Fils
British abstract and contemporary art.

www.gimpelfils.com

University of the Arts

Has a gallery showing work by current
students and alumni. Café inside.

www.arts.ac.uk

This tramble ends at Bond Street
Station

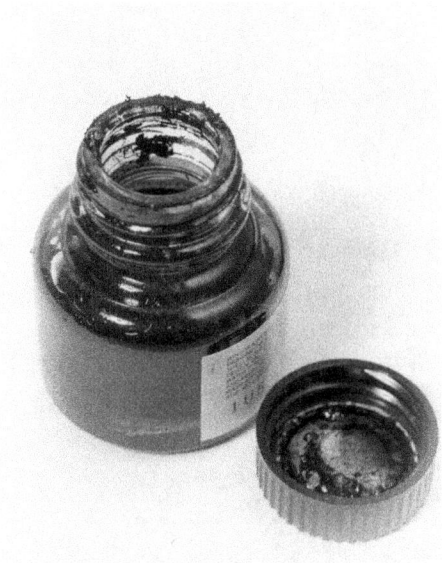

t7 Waterloo

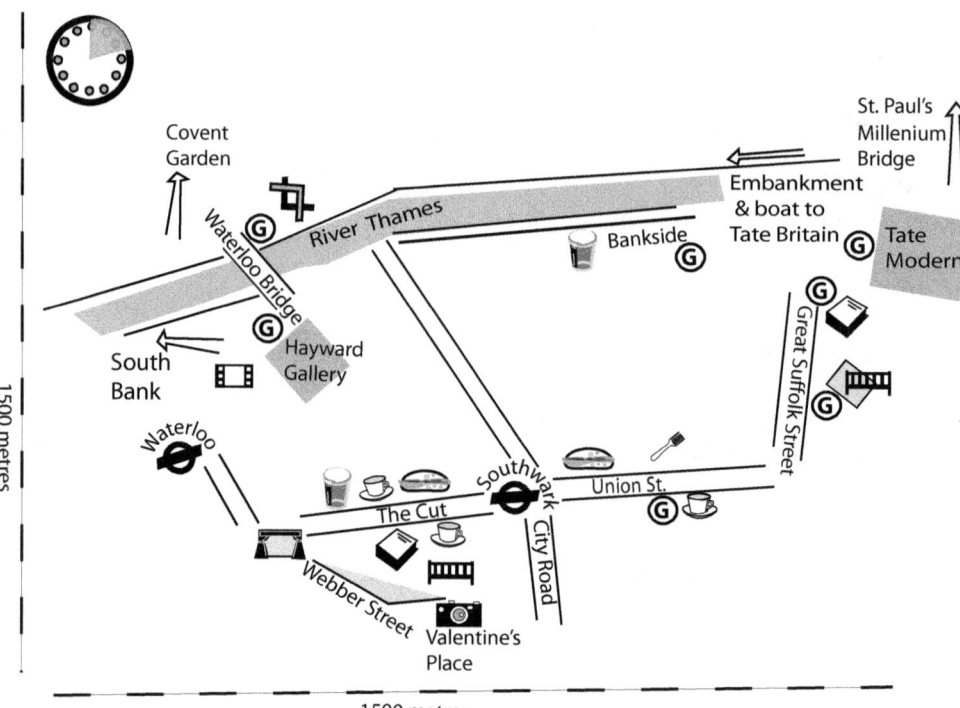

St. Paul's
Millenium
Bridge

Covent
Garden

River Thames

Embankment
& boat to
Tate Britain

Bankside

Tate
Modern

Waterloo Bridge

Great Suffolk Street

Hayward
Gallery

South
Bank

Waterloo

1500 metres

Southwark

Union St.

The Cut

City Road

Webber Street

Valentine's
Place

1500 metres

Waterloo - Bankside *t7*

By Boat from Tate Britain (see t2 Pimlico p14) *or across* Millennium Bridge from St. Paul's. (join from Farringdon or Holborn t8 p.88)

Depart from the grand station along *The Cut*. Beneath railway bridges to *Union Street*
Arrive at the Bankside powerhouse Tate Modern.

Extend this tramble by crossing the Thames on *Millennium Bridge* to the foot of St. Paul's Cathedral

Arriving at Waterloo Station
At the entrance sculpture by **Philip Jackson** of **Terence Cuneo** (1907-96). Cueno. Cueno is noted for paintings of railways.Other notable sculptures by Philip Jackson include the World Cup Winning EnglandFootball team captain Bobby Moore outside Wembley Stadium, and HM the Queen Mother Memorial in The Mall.

It is impossible to ignore the draw of the South Bank. *A refreshing stroll* Browse through second-hand books outside the British Film Institute before stepping inside the **Hayward Gallery**

Venture past ***Oxo Tower*** and the **Globe Theatre** restaurant to **Tate Modern.** To be able to reel off such a list of major landmarks so easily shows the depth of culture available on this historic stretch of the Thames. Still the most direct way to access London's arts and culture, and a great way to clear your mind in such a busy city.

These are major sites to return to frequently, trambles are about discovering smaller places. Like finding your way behind the scenes on a grand film set

From **Waterloo Station**

This tramble leads you behind the river to discover notable smaller places of interest, along the way to major spaces.

Turn right then left onto **The Cut.**
A quick detour for photo enthusiasts:

Up Webber St on to **Valentine Place**

Silverprint

Specialist in photographic printing materials, paper, cameras and photo books. *Silverprint* continues to support a much loved disappearing art.

Back on **Webber Street** into *Ufford St through* a small park .
Continue into Mitre Street, back to The Cut.

The Cut

Linking Waterloo to Southwark The Cut has developed in to a thriving mixture of cafes, small shops and restaurants around the **Old Vic** and **Young Vic** theatres.

Plenty of interesting stops along *The Cut* for pre-theatre enteertainment. Excellent restaurants and cafes sit alongside camping equipment, florist and barber shop.

Calder's

Specialist theatrical bookshop that holds poetry readings and performances, small stage at the rear.

Cross Blackfriars Road to *Union Street* for **Jerwood Space**.

Jerwood provide rehearsal and performance space, sponsor several art prizes and assist younger artists to gain recognition. Including drawing, photography, sculpture and portrait prizes. The quality of the work on display is consistently high.

www.jerwoodspace.co.uk

Down Great Suffolk Street, into *Hopton Stree*t

Purdy & Hicks
Contemporary British and Irish painting and photography alongside international artists

www.purdyhicks.com

Modern Art Bookstore
An abundance of exhibition catalogues and large format art books for collectors.

Bankside Gallery
The Royal Watercolour Society and The Royal Society of Painter-Printmakers. Beautiful variety of watercolours and prints. Exhibitions, talks and events.

www.banksidegallery.com

Complete this tramble at **Tate Modern**

TATE MODERN

Tate Modern has been open just over a decade. It's hard to consider it opened so recently, since it has offered many memorable displays and has become such a constant and prominent feature on the south side of the river.

As Tate continue to extend the galleries for more displays from late 20th Century and current artists, it becomes clear that Tate Modern has just scratched the surface. There is much more of the collection to be uncovered and put on display. A very exciting prospect for all modern art enthusiasts.

www.tate.org.uk

Spitalfields to Smithfield *t*8

Join this tramble from Tate Modern *(t7)*

Cross the Thames on the Millennium footbridge, past St Paul's Cathedral *Up* Foster Lane to join this tramble on Gresham St, at the Guildhall Art Gallery and Museum.

Extended tramble begins **at the Whitechapel Art Gallery** (see t9 also) Recently expanded, superb gallery space with contemporary art and photography displays.

t8 Spitalfields

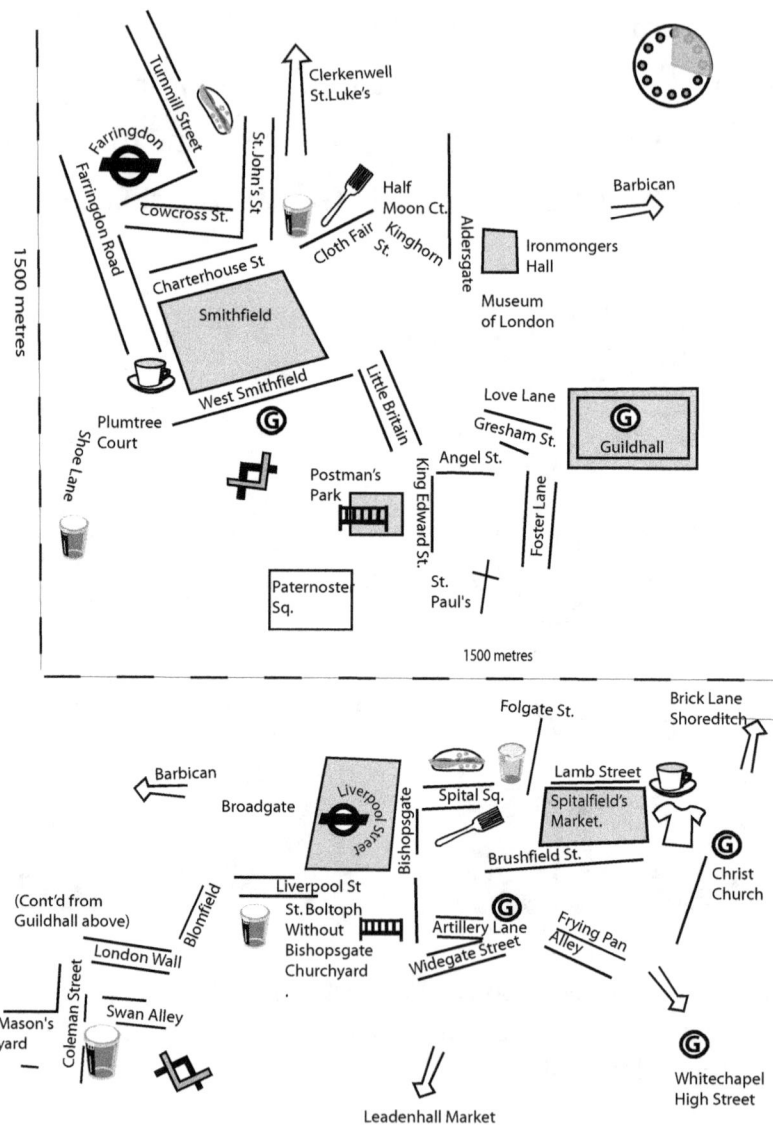

Nicholas Hawksmoor worked as clerk to Sir Christopher Wren on the re-building of Kensington Palace, and St Paul's Cathedral. His most recognised work as architect are the West Towers of Westminster Abbey. Alongside ChristChurch Hawsmoor designed five otherchurches across London including; St Annes Limehouse, St. George in The East, St Georges Bloomsbury, St Mary Woolnoth, St Alfege Greenwich all built between 1711 and 1730. Money to build these and other churches built in London at this time was raised by an increase in tax on coal passed by Parliament in 1711.

Down Whitechapel Road, Osborn St, on to Fournier St Cross Commercial Road *into Old Spitalfields*

On **Fournier Street**
The *Hawksmoor* baroque Christ Church completed in 1727
inside is **The Rectory** gallery
(see also Curwen p38)

Around Spitalfield's Market
On *Folgate Street*
The Water Poets pub overshadowed by huge office blocks

Lamb St
Take tea at **TeaSmith**

Artillery Lane
Raven Row Gallery
Contemporary art displayed
in two Rococo style Hugenot houses
www.ravenrow.org

*Down **Brushfield Street***
S&M sausage and mash,
A.Gold which is a fine deli, that also sells old fashioned sweets.

Two tiny streets worth a quick look. On **Widegate Street** a series of ceramic relief sculptures bakers by **Phillip Lindsey Clark (1926)** above a baker's shop.

About the Artist

Phillip Lindsey - Clark

Born in London 1889.
Studied at Cheltenham from 1905 to 1910, and at the City and Guilds School, Kensington from 1910 to 1914. Served in the army during the first world war. Continued studying after the war. Went on to create a series of similar relief sculptures at churches and memorials across the UK.. One of Clark's best known works is the war memorial at St. Saviour's Church in Southwark.

utside Liverpool Street Station

**hildren of the
inder Transport**

his commission is one of a three part series
Frank Miesler. There are similar sculptures
utside stations in Berlin and Gdansk. Dedi-
ted in gratitude to the people of Britain
ho helped save the lives of 10,000 mainly
wish children who fled from Nazi perse-
tion in 1938-39. In the months between
istalnacht (Nov 10 1938) and the start of
WII, children, of which some were babies
rried by children, left without their
arents from Austria, Poland, and Czecho-
ovakia to safety in Great Britain.

About
the
Artist

Frank
Meisler

Cross Bishopsgate at *St Boltoph's Church through* St Boltoph's Passage

Benches for a welcome rest.
Bathhouse bar restaurant housed in a beautiful Turkish bathhouse, sitting in the shadows of the city office buildings.

Turn left down *Old Broad* St,
on to *London Wall.*

View to the left of the Bank of England

Turn down **Coleman St** through *Mason's Yard* towards the Guildhall.

lumbian artist Botero's
ulptures of human and animal
ures noted for their
aggerated proportions.

tirical portraits of human
d political references. In 1993

tero exhibited some sculptures
ong the Champs Elysees, Paris. The
st time a non French artist had
ne so.

 has also exhibited in New York,
icago, Tokyo and Madrid.

About the Artist

Fernando Botero

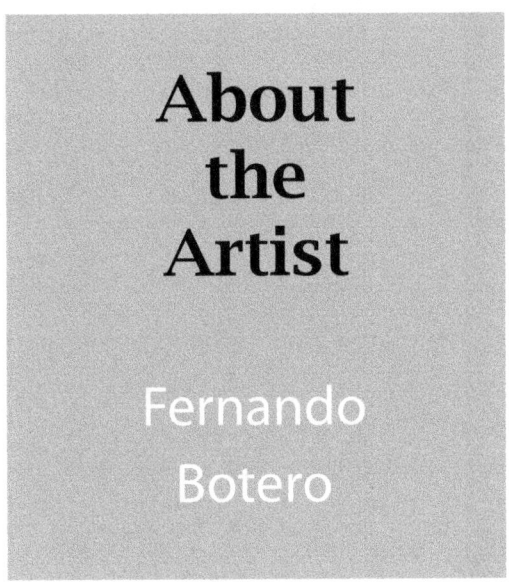

change Square

e Broadgate Venus

ormous 5-ton reclining nude
ated by **Fernando Botero** placed in
hange Square

Into **Guildhall Art Gallery**

The City of London began collecting works of art in the seventeenth century, commissioned portraits of the judges appointed to assess property claims in the wake of the Great Fire of London of 1666. Its collection now comprises 4,000 works of art ranging from portraits of kings and queens to depictions of important naval battles, from period views of historic London to the work of contemporary artists. The City of London's collection has concentrated on London subjects. There is also a large landscape by John Constable, Salisbury Cathedral from the Meadows. Contemporary pictures by younger artists living and working in London, purchased through the Lord Mayor's Art Award exhibitions.

The original Library at Guildhall was founded in the 1420s.
A major public reference library which specialises in the history of London.
It also houses the largest clockmaker's museum in the world.
a unique exhibition tracing the development of clocks and watches through the centuries.

Exit Guildhall on Gresham Street
View on to the Swiss Re Tower

(At the end of Gresham Street, turn left for St Paul's Cathedral)

About the Artist

George Frederic Watts
(1817-1904)

Postman's Park

Straight ahead past *St. Bartholomew's Medical College* on Little Britain, King Edward Street and Angel Street.

Inside the park a touching memorial created by *George Frederic Watts* in 1900. Dedicated to those who sacrificed their own lives to save others. Decorative tiles tell of heroic acts by ordinary people. A humbling yet inspirational monument to human kindness.

One of the most significant artists of the Victorian age. A prolific painter of over 300 portraits, *a sculptor, and landscape painter.*

Many portraits were given the National Portrait Gallery, and the Whitechapel Gallery. Later as sculptor significant works across London include Physical Energy in Kensington on Gardens, see p.9
In 1884 he was the first living artist to have a solo exhibition at the Metropolitan Museum of Art, New York

To learn more about Watts visit Watts Gallery in Guildford has recently been refurbishded and re-opens to the public in June 2011.
It can be reached by rail from Waterloo Station Details of a circularwalk from the train station to the gallery are on the website.

www.wattsgallery.org.uk

West Smithfield

Smithfield Gallery
Open for exhibitions and hire for events.

www.smithfieldgallery.com

The Nocturne Cycle Race
In West Smithfield in June there is a spectacular night time cycle race, *Nocturne*
From dusk into the night Britain's top professional cyclists speed past silently like bats around the market place. Spectators gather outside pubs on the pavement to watch the action. Restaurants join in the fun, decorating the windows and walls with bicycles. Well worth a visit.

Cloth Fair

Complete this tramble at **Cloth Fair** Where *Sir John Betjeman* once lived.*(See also t4 and t11)*

Options:
Head up to t10 Clerkenwell p.99
Down to St Paul's
t7 Bankside and Tate Modern
or
Across to t4 Holborn & Bloomsbury. p.39

My favourite neighbourhood

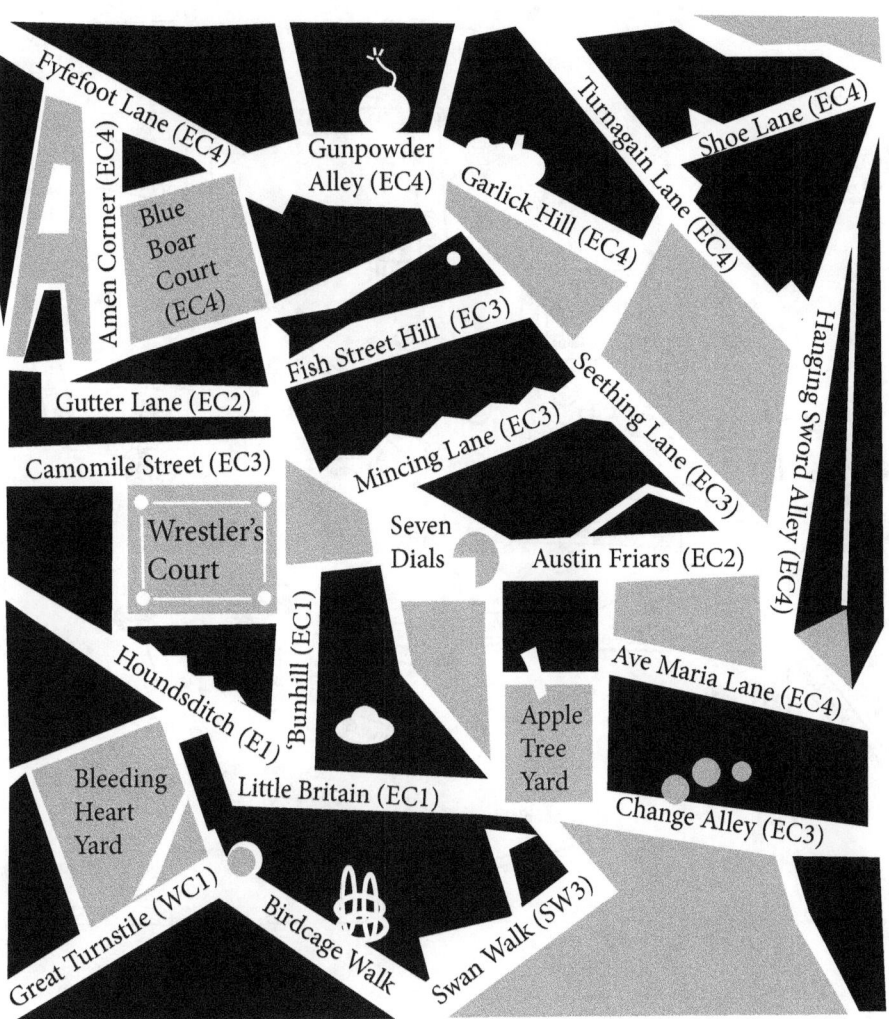

Actual London street names in a fictitious neighbourhood.

t9 Shoreditch

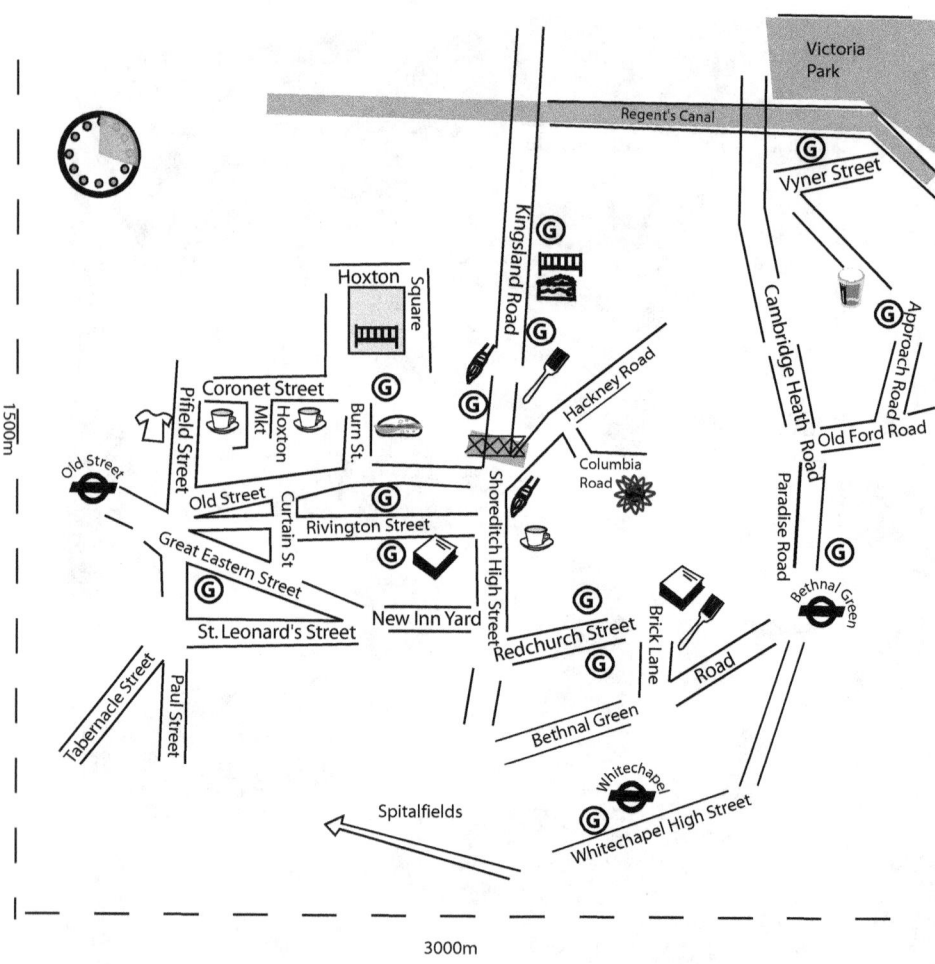

*t***9**

Shoreditch to Bethnal Green

Letters painted by Ben Eine

Whether it's the excellent Whitechapel Art Gallery, or one of the smaller galleries, the depth and variety of art in this area of London cannot be matched. More artists live and work in this area than in any other part of London.

Ben Eine has become known for his brightly coloured lettering in city spaces. notably for his alphabet lettering on shop shutters in Shoreditch and Brick Lane.

Beneath the brightly coloured archway into **Shoreditch High Street.**

Cowling & Wilcox
Art suppliers

Time for Tea
On Sunday enjoy afternoon tea and cake. Doubles as a tiny cinema.

Syd's Coffee Stall on *Shoreditch High Street* since 1919.
Take a moment to admire the tiled arches of the *Wells Commercial Ironworks* opposite.

Walk up Shoreditch High Street
Cross onto **Kingsland Road**

Under the iron railway bridge
In the shadows the discreet entrance to **Seventeen** a small art space, with a second space tucked away in the basement.

The PrintSpace
Europe's first walk-in DIY professional photographic printing lab. Launched in 2007 the printspace occupies two floors of exhibition space, retouching booths, and large format printers.

Further up on Kingsland Road

Flowers East
A major contemporary art space.

www.flowerseast.com
(see also – Cork Street t6 p60)

Next door to Flowers East

Mathmos
Founded by Edward Craven-Walker
Inventor of the Lava lamp in 1963,
household favourite of the 1970s
still selling today.

Eats
There are a couple Vietnamese restaurants along here; Hung Viet, Mien Tay,
and Sons Que Café. ***Troy*** a pattisserie
with it's handsome carved wooden sign.

View of Tower 42 (*Nat West* Tower*)*

Return on **Kingsland Road**

The Geffrye Museum

Furniture, textiles, paintings and objects displayed in series of period rooms from 1600 to the present day.

Occasionally open to the public is an 18th Century almshouse fully restored to it's original condition, offers a glimpse into the lives of London's poor and elderly.

Allow 2-3 hours to visit the museum and grounds. There is also a restaurant.

In front of the museum there is a scented garden with benches.

www.geffrye-museum.org.uk

Back down **Shoreditch High Street**

Down on **Great Eastern Street**
is a marvellous figurehead that looks like
an alien chewing on a pound coin up on
a wall. I would love to know who put it
there.

Cross on to **Bethnal Green Road**

Up Ebor Street
Into **Redchurch Street**

Brick Lane and surrounds

I could have filled this book with the
variety of creative outputs in Brick Lane
It is a creative hang out and home to
many artists and studios. A couple of
introductions to Brick Lane which are
on the edge of this tramble.
Spend time exploring the wide variety
of shops, cafes, and restaurants..

The approach gallery

an excellent space above the approach tavern
47 Approach Road, Bethnal Green

www.theapproach.co.uk

The approach gallery is not continuously open throughout the year, so please check for opening times.

While the area is changing rapidly with the introduction of new rail links, I hope it can continue to retain it's rough and ready edge with a mix of artists and residents alongside small family businesses. All seem to thrive on each other's presence, any further modernisation may lose the creative energy.

Get Involved &
The Concrete Hermit

At this point I would like to mention *Get Involved*. *Get* Involved was a club night which approached a different designer or image-maker to produce the promotional poster for each month's event.

They recently held an exhibition at *the Concrete Hermit*.
Link on their web site to Record Shops
(See note on Mooching earlier on)

www.getinvolvedclub.com/recordshops/london/

www.concretehermit.com

Café
Collection

An increasing number of cafés, some of which have even been given permission to have seats and serve food outside.

Exit Farringdon Station on Turnmill Street.

Start with a peanut butter bagel from Meze opposite the station before heading up Benjamin Street. Clerkenwell used to be the centre for sign writers, typographers, publishers and printers.

t10 Farringdon

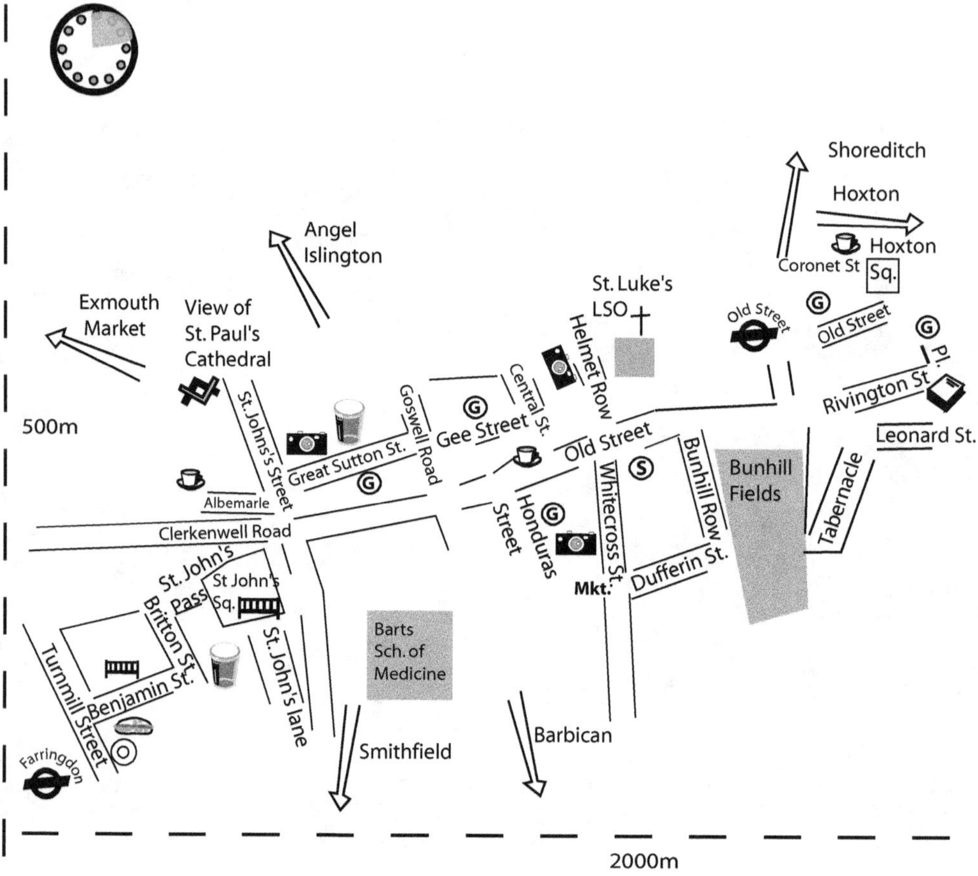

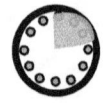

Shoreditch
Hoxton
Hoxton
Sq.
Coronet St
Angel
Islington
St. Luke's
LSO
Exmouth
Market
View of
St. Paul's
Cathedral
Old Street
Old Street
Pl.
Helmet Row
Central St.
Rivington St
Leonard St.
500m
St. Johns's Street
Goswell Road
Gee Street
Old Street
Great Sutton St.
Bunhill Row
Bunhill
Fields
Albemarle
Whitecross St.
Tabernacle
Clerkenwell Road
Honduras
Street
Dufferin St.
St. John's
Pass
St John's
Sq.
Mkt.
Britton St.
Barts
Sch. of
Medicine
Turnmill Street
St. John's lane
Benjamin St.
Barbican
Smithfield
Farringdon
2000m

St. John's Museum	101
Marsden Woo	102
Magnum	102
HOST	103
Rivington Place	105
YCN	105

On to **Benjamin Street**,
A small garden on the left hand side.

Left into **Britton Street**.

The Jerusalem Tavern
The tavern dates from 1720. One of the
open every weekday for meals, coffee
A range of St. Peter's ales brewed at the
Suffolk brewery.

www.stpetersbrewery.co.uk/london

At the side of the Jerusalem Tavern cut
through *St John's Passage* to *St John's
Square.*

St. John's Museum

The Museum and Library of the Order
of St. John housed in a16th century
gatehouse.

St. John's Gate, formed the southern
entrance to a priory covering 10-acres
of Clerkenwell in Medieval times.
Key features include gallery with an
interactive timeline.

www.sja.org.uk

Cross St. John's Road
Cut through Albermarle Street

St. Paul's Cathedral *pops it's head over the horizon as you cross the street.*

In to **Great Sutton Street**
Pass Metro photo processing lab and the **Slaughtered Lamb** pub.

Marsden Woo Gallery

Fine art, applied art, ceramics and sculpture on two floors.

www.marsdenwoo.com

Cross Goswell road into **Gee Street**

At the end of Gee Street it is worth taking time to find no.. 63 the **Magnum** London office. The world's most prestigious photographic agency formed by four photographers - Robert Capa, Henri Cartier-Bresson, George Rodger and David "Chim" Seymour in 1947. Always has excellent photography on display. It is discreetly tucked on the ground floor of an office building.

www.magnumphotos.com

Down onto **Old Street**

Look Mama No Hands!

Café bar for cycling enthusiasts, with cycle racks, and Cycling races live on screen.

Cross to **Honduras Street**

HOST Gallery

Photojournalism and documentary photography

www.hostgallery.co.uk

A little further up
on **Helmet Row** to view **St Luke's Church** now home to the London Symphony Orchestra.

A diversion onto **Whitecross Street** for the market

Halfway down ***Whitecross St***, *turn left* onto **Dufferin Street**.

At the end of *Dufferin Street*

Bunhill Row
John Wesley's House and Museum.

John Wesley
and The Wesley Museum

Grade I listed Georgian architecture
Wesley's Chapel Built in 1778 by John
Wesley, the founder of Methodism.
The Chapel was his London base and
replaced his previous London Chapel,
The Foundary which stood about 200
yards away.

Take a look inside the elegant simple
chapel with it's beautiful stained glass.
Designed by the architect George Dance
the Younger, surveyor to the City of
London.

Bunhill Fields burial ground
Memorials for ***Daniel Defoe*** and
William Blake amongst other notable
names.

Leaving Bunhill fields, cross **City Road**
on to **St Leonard's Stree**t

Turn up **Paul Street.**

Cross **Great Eastern Street**
On to **Rivington Street**

Rivington Place

Designed by architect David Adjaye OBE. The first new build gallery since the Hayward Gallery *(see T7 Waterloo)* in 1968. Home to two charitable organisations; Iniva -The Institute Of International Visual Arts, and Autograph ABP, for education in contemporary art and photography.

www.rivingtonplace.org

YCN
Young Creative Network

Opposite Rivington Place another space worth mentioning is YCN -Young Creative Network. Supporting young designers with space to work and exhibit. YCN create projects to showcase emerging talent; as well as producing design, campaigns and other communication for clients. The ground floor is a gallery and shop.

www.ycnonline.com

Pitfield Street

Bookart Bookshop
Sells artist's books and small press publications

Cottage Café,
Serve traditional homemade food.

Ca4LA – from Japan
Specialising in affordable designer hats. Over 3,000 different styles.

Orhan Tailor
Bespoke Tailor for men and women

Off **Pitfield Street,** *on to* **Coronet Street** *and* **Hoxton Market**
A fine square to sit out in.

Outside **The Juggler Café**

A sculpture of a Juggler
by *Simon Stringer*

Born in Devon, studied Fine Art in
South Africa, Simon Stringer returned
to the UK to complete an MA in
Sculpture at the Royal Academy.
The Juggler was commisioned
by Hackney Council in 1994.
Series of shows followed and in 2000
commissioned by Tate Modern to create
bronzes for the Educational Dept.
Stringer has continued to work from
North London on commissions for
schools, gardens, and group shows
around England.

www.simonstringer.com

Back on **Coronet Street**
Into **Hoxton Square**

White Cube

One of London's most influential
galleries. This larger gallery opened in
2000, following the success of the original White Cube Gallery in Duke Street,
established in 1993. This has been
replaced by the gallery at Mason's Yard
in the West End *(see t6 St.James's)*

www.whitecube.com

About the Artist

Simon Stringer

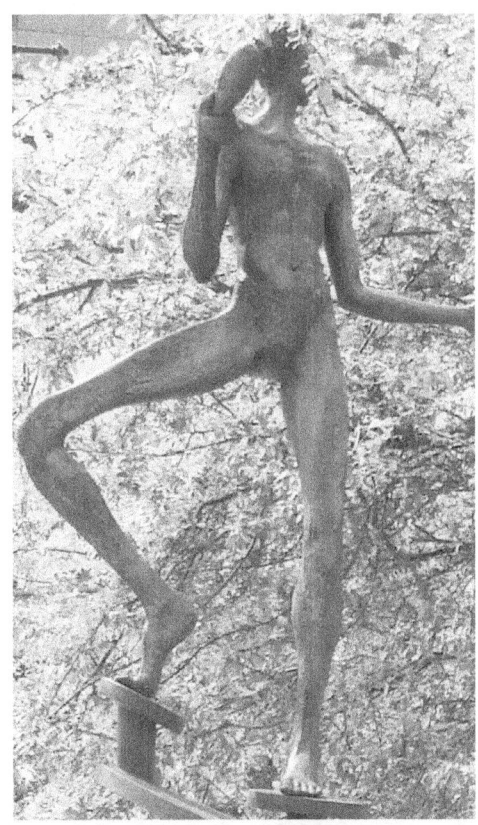

Juggling figure
by Simon Stringer

Islington t11

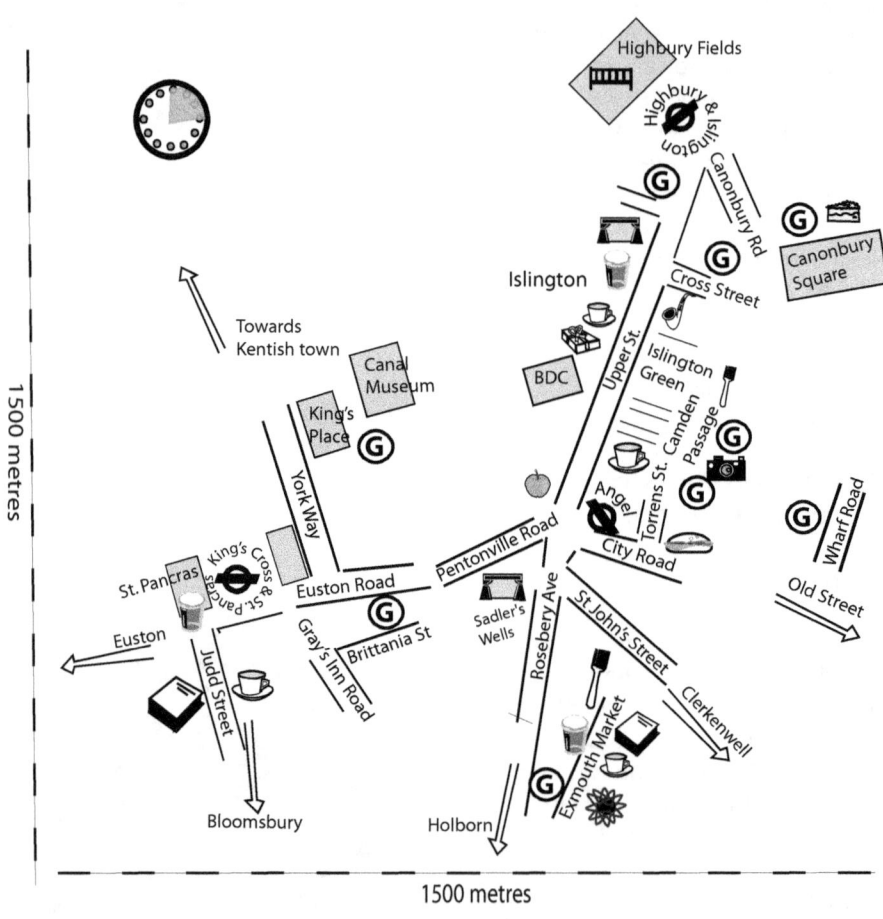

*t*11
Islington

Highbury & Islington to Holborn taking in Exmouth Market
Extended tramble includes King's Cross & St Pancras.

From the elegant Estorick gallery through arts and antique markets behind busy Upper Street, down to cafés and finishing at Lincoln's Inn Fields.

Estorick Collection

Eric Estorick (1913-93)

The American sociologist and writer. Eric Estorick was an intellectual who in his late teens fell in love with modern art, and began to form a collection which is now world famous. Began to collect works of art when he come to live in England after the Second World War. In 1970 the Italian Republic presented Estorick the honour of Commendatore for his services in promoting Italian art. Estorick set up the Eric and Salome Estorick Foundation, to which he donated all his Italian works. The Georgian house at 39a Canonbury Square, Islington, was refurbished to display the collection, café and shop. It features paintings by Futurist's: Giacomo Balla, Umberto Boccioni, Carlo Carrà, Gino Severini, Amedeo Modigliani.

www.estorickcollection.com

Sculpture in the Estorick garden Lauren, by Edward Dutkiewicz

Off Upper Street **Compton Terrace**

Union Chapel

Host to many up and coming bands, musicians, and comedians.

The Friends of Union Chapel helped restore and preserve Union Chapel, Islington, and organise a variety of activities in the building. The Friends were founded in 1982 as a response to the threat of demolition of the building.
Church members, local residents and lovers of heritage and architecture came together successfully to fight off demolition. They are now trying to raise money to restore the chapel tower.

www.unionchapel.org.uk

Up **Canonbury Lane**
on to **Upper Street**
Turn left in to *Cross Street*
& Shillingford Street

Cross Street
Fancy boutiques, interior decorators,
and a music shop.
Cross Street Gallery
Formerly a bakery it now holds a
collection of modern British
and contemporary art.

www.crossstreetgallery.com

Continue on Upper Street

The Almeida Theatre
Classics from the British, American and
Irish repertoire, foreign classics and new
plays. The Almeida Islington is a unique
arena for public performance.
Previously a music hall, and Salvation
Army Citadel. Refurbished in 2003.

The King's Head Theatre
Opened in 1970 the first pub theatre
founded in England since the days of
Shakespeare. previously a boxing ring
and a pool hall. Various elements of the
theatre, including the red velvet curtains
and theatre lamps have been recyled
from other famous venues. It continues
to promote new and exciting creative
talent.

Hart Gallery
Painters, Sculptors, Printmakers
& Ceramicists
www.hartgallery.co.uk

Continue towards Islington Green

John Maine studied at the West of England College of Art from 1960 to 1964 before moving to London to attend the Royal College of Art until 1967.
He then set up a sculpture studio in Shoreditch. First solo exhibition held at the Serpentine Gallery in 1972. He has since shown regularly in Britain and abroad.

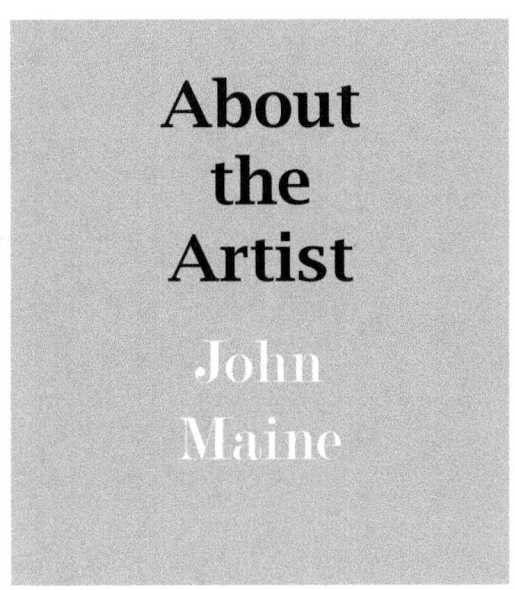

About the Artist

John Maine

granite memorial wreath (2006) arved from one solid piece of stone, :ans gracefully on a stone wall in lington Green A replacement for ne existing war memorial, a tradi-onal obelisk which had stood on ne site since 1918, as the focus for :membrance services.

The Screen on the Green

Another excellent local cinema part of the *Everyman* group of cinemas, also in Hampstead and Baker Street.

Business Design Centre

For the past few years in January the London art fair has been held at the Business Design Centre. It is a good way to get an overview of galleries, and some affordable art can be found here.

www.londonartfair.co.uk

Cross Upper St

Across the Green
Behind Upper Street

Camden Passage
Collectables, antiques, books,
and vintage clothes.

The Breakfast Club
Friendly tiny yellow cube cafe has
everything you want for brunch
and lunch including English
breakfast, pancakes, and
smoothies.
Also in Hoxton, by White Cube ,
and also soon to be in Spitalfield.

Rock Archive
Rock and pop photography

Japanese Gallery
Traditional drawings and Manga
animation cells.

Out of Camden Passage

Into **Torrens Street**

Candid Arts

A gallery that supports up and coming artists. A courtyard café and another on the second floor. Two Victorian warehouses provide exhibition space, and galleries. Twenty artists studios, conference and screening rooms, rehearsal spaces to promote the arts and arts education, with special emphasis placed on helping newly graduated artists and designers in their first years out of college.

www.candidarts.com

*Cross **City Road** and **Goswell Road***

On to **St John's Road**
(see Clerkenwell t10 also)

Tramble past the **Red Lion Theatre** onto **Rosebury Avenue**

Sadler's Wells Theatre
Dedicated to bringing the very best international and UK dance to London audiences. The first Sadler's Wells theatre opened in 1683. The current building opened in 1998.

Down past Finsbury Town Hall
A fading elegant Victorian building now a dance studio.

Exmouth Market

Behind Rosebury Avenue off Tysoe Street.
A laid back row of cafés and restaurants.
Ideal for sitting out in the sunshine.
Beer and snacks at **Café Kick**
a tiny café bar with table football
Or enjoy some serious Spanish food at

Moro friendly service, fantastic food
& atmosphere.

Inked
Art gallery for original prints

www. inked-art.com

Pod an arty garden shop with flowers,
gifts and accessories.

Clerkenwell Tales bookshop

From **Exmouth Market**

Down Grays Inn Road
Grays Inn Gardens
(only open between 12-2.30pm)

Turn on to **Theobalds Road**
Exit on *Jockeys Fields*
Into **Brownlow Street**

Turn right on **Holborn**

Down tiny **Great Turnstile passageway**

Leads into
Lincoln's Inn Fields

There are benches, including a grand
sculptural seat in the park dedicated to
Margaret Macdonald wife of Ramsay
Macdonald the first British Labour Prime
Minister.

Sir John Soane's Museum

Sir John Soane demolished
12,13, and 14 on the North side
of Lincoln's Inn Fields, from 1792
to 1823-24 and re-designed the
house to live in and as a setting
for his antiquities and works of art.
On his appointment as Professor
of Architecture at the Royal
Academy in 1806 he arranged the
books, casts and models for easy
access. The 'Academy of
Architecture' continues to
maintain the Museum, as far
as possible in the state in which
it was left at the time of Soane's
death in 1837.

www.soane.org

Exit the square on Remnant Street on to Kingsway

Cross into **St. Giles** *(see t5)*
or
Turn right for Holborn Station

Cross over Kingsway on to **High Holborn** for one of my favourite pubs in central London

Princess Louise

Fully restored and preserved in all it's original Victorian splendour. Beautiful decorative mirrors, and stained glass. A narrow bar and staircases on either side take you up to a small bar upstairs.

Take a pint and a well earned rest!

From here you can tramble on to **Bloomsbury** *(See t4 page 40)*

Galleries